Our
Auntie Rosa

Our Auntie Rosa

The Family of Rosa Parks Remembers
Her Life and Lessons

SHEILA McCAULEY KEYS

with Eddie B. Allen, Jr.

JEREMY P. TARCHER/PENGUIN
a member of Penguin Group (USA)
New York

JEREMY P. TARCHER/PENGUIN
Published by the Penguin Group
Penguin Group (USA) LLC
375 Hudson Street
New York, New York 10014

USA · Canada · UK · Ireland · Australia
New Zealand · India · South Africa · China

penguin.com
A Penguin Random House Company

Most Tarcher/Penguin books are available at special quantity discounts for bulk purchase for sales
promotions, premiums, fund-raising, and educational needs. Special books or book excerpts also
can be created to fit specific needs. For details, write: Special.Markets@us.penguingroup.com.

Library of Congress Cataloging-in-Publication Data
Keys, Sheila McCauley.
Our Auntie Rosa : the family of Rosa Parks remembers her life and lessons /
Sheila McCauley Keys with Eddie B. Allen, Jr.
p.   cm.
ISBN 978-0-399-17389-9
1. Parks, Rosa, 1913–2005—Family.   2. African American women civil rights workers—
Alabama—Montgomery—Biography.   3. Civil rights workers—Alabama—Montgomery—
Biography.   4. McCauley family.   5. Keys, Sheila McCauley—Family.   6. African Americans—
Michigan—Detroit—Biography.   7. African American political activists—Michigan—Biography.
8. Older women—Michigan—Detroit—Biography.   9. Montgomery (Ala.)—Biography.
10. Detroit (Mich.)—Biography.   I. Allen, Eddie B.   II. Title.   III. Title: Family of Rosa Parks
remembers her life and lessons.
F334.M753K49   2014   2014038463
323.092—dc23
[B]

Printed in the United States of America
1   3   5   7   9   10   8   6   4   2

BOOK DESIGN BY NICOLE LAROCHE

CONTENTS

For Sylvester and Daisy McCauley

Our Auntie Rosa

4/12/93
Rosa Parks
with love and best wishes
to my niece Susan
and children

THE WOMAN WE KNEW

Coming from such a simple background in rural Tuskegee, Alabama, Rosa Louise McCauley probably never imagined she would one day be known around the world. Born to our grandparents James and Leona McCauley on February 4, 1913, Auntie Rosa was introduced to struggles and poverty long before she would be introduced to foreign dignitaries. The separation of our grandparents when she was still just a girl added to her responsibilities at home, including helping look after her younger brother, our father, Sylvester. It would be decades later before she earned even more responsibility, including her most honorific title, "Mother of the Movement," when she defied legal segregation on a Southern bus line in 1955.

After largely disappearing from the public once she moved North, our aunt became more widely acknowledged as a hero. She went on to receive the Presidential Medal of Freedom; a spot on *TIME* magazine's "100 Most Influential People of the 20th Century" list; forty-three honorary doctorate degrees; and streets, buildings, and monuments named in her tribute. Throughout all this, she still found her way to our weddings, birthday parties, and other family events. She was there encouraging and helping us throughout our lives. To the world, she was Rosa Parks, but to us, she was, simply and wonderfully, Auntie Rosa. This book is about the woman we knew.

—Deborah Ann Ross

Rosalind Elaine Bridgeforth and son, Alan Bridgeforth

Asheber Macharia; wife, Najma Wilson;
and daughter, Zakiya Watts

Rhea McCauley and daughter, Edria Fussello

Robert McCauley

Susan McCauley; sons Sean and Broderick;
and daughter, Whitney

Shirley McCauley and son, Paul Jenkins

Sheila McCauley Keys and sons Terrence Jamal Keys
and Thomas McCauley Keys

Richard McCauley

Lonnie McCauley, son of Sylvester McCauley Jr. (deceased)

Marc McCauley, son of Mary McCauley

February 2015

Painting by Asheber Macharia

PLEASED TO MEET YOU, MRS. PARKS

In a peculiar way, I felt that I knew her well.

We spoke only twice, and then I'd imagine no more than twenty or thirty words between us from both events combined: the first when she awarded me a scholarship bearing her name and the second after a home invasion by a man who actually called that name aloud, asking, "Aren't you Rosa Parks?" before he hit her in the face and robbed her.

Maybe it was just that same comfort I've often experienced with women who fell into my grandmother's peer group. I've noticed this, increasingly, since "Mama Harriet," Harriet Crain—born, like Rosa McCauley, in Alabama, just months earlier—died in 1996.

Yet the truth was, despite the fact that a newspaper colleague of mine was her private photographer, and despite my years as a Wayne State University "Rosa Parks Scholar" in her adopted hometown of Detroit, I knew Mrs. Parks no more on the personal level than any of her distant admirers. I felt privileged, of course, to shake her hand at the scholarship ceremony and pose with her for a quick photo. A few years later, I found myself telephoning her assistant from my desk at the Ohio newspaper where I worked when I needed a quote or two for my story about the heinous attack Joseph Skipper committed against the then-eighty-one-year-old "Mother Parks," as she was known to neighbors. After promising that I'd be brief, since she was tired and recovering from the ordeal, I was connected with Mrs. Parks, who told me she was okay.

"Things have worked out well," I remember her saying in our two-minute interview.

During our last encounter, she spoke no words at all. On that day in 2005, I'd been asked to cover her funeral for the AOL Black Voices website. I heard President Bill Clinton tell the story of how, as liberal white kids in Arkansas, he and his friends decided they didn't have to ride in the front of the bus upon learning that Mrs. Parks had refused to stand and ride in the back. I watched as she was saluted in a manner befitting heads of state by a string of high-profile dignitaries, including Detroit Mayor Kwame Kilpatrick and then-senator Barack Obama. It was a most moving day, which concluded as onlookers lined the streets awaiting her funeral procession to the burial ground. Calls of "We love you, Rosa!" were absent of the tone of disrespect most people who were raised like I was often associate with addressing elders by first name. What it really spoke to was the familiar kinship these folks, who probably knew her even less than I did, had developed with our city's best-known freedom fighter.

So it was with a renewed excitement that I first met Mrs. Parks' niece Sheila Keys in August 2012. As she entered the office of her family's lawyer, Lawrence Pepper, I immediately spotted a resemblance to her aunt in her eyes and nose, although she was much taller and more statuesque. During the course of our meeting, I also caught a glimpse of what Sheila and her siblings have decided to share with the world in *Our Auntie Rosa*—the familiar smile often found stretched across Mrs. Parks' slender face in photo after photo, but in these shots her smile was accompanied by the smiles of her loved ones. Woven between these intimate images were words and language only family members could construct about a favorite relative. I hadn't truly known Mrs. Parks in life, but I would get to know her now.

In making your own acquaintance with the loving mother figure, who never shrank behind her frontline-warrior legend status, don't be surprised to read stories that remind you of your own cherished elders and ancestors. Sylvester McCauley's children serve as guides on a nostalgic, but enlightening, tour through the many years when Mrs. Parks was an influential presence in their lives, particularly after their mother died in 1981. Within these pages, Mrs. Parks' personal humanity emerges, drawing a stark contrast to the bespectacled, solemn-faced outlaw depicted in her infamous 1955 Montgomery County Jail booking photo. I felt privileged, as I hope you will, to learn more about the lady whose soft facial features flicker onto our TVs during Black History Month and on Dr. King's holiday.

The bonds described here have survived decades, withstanding physical separation and geographic distance. This rare collection of the combined memories and reflections of Mrs. Parks' closest living kin allows us to join the family in celebrating her spirit 100 years after her birth, and beyond.

—EDDIE B. ALLEN, JR.

January 2014

Detroit

Family

·····································

Don't make a fuss about me. I'm just your auntie.

—ROSA PARKS,
civil rights activist

The Interview

Among her nephews and nieces, she never talked much about That Day.

In many ways, she was like a firefighter who rushes out of a blazing structure with a limp body in his arms, just as the roof collapses, and then says, "I was only doing my job."

Neither, for some reason, did her surrogate children tend to broach the subject, directly, even as they read about it in history class. She once told Ebony *magazine that she refused to give up her seat because she was "tired" and her "feet hurt." In other interviews, Mrs. Parks said she was tired all right; tired of being pushed around. Yet if private chats about the civil rights movement showed signs of turning toward her, or if she thought a topic might lead one of her young relatives to ask what occurred on the Cleveland Avenue bus line, she would just flash that disarming smile and reply, "That's not important right now."*

Then, decades later, she found herself at home with only Shirley, the niece who, as a little girl, became so masterful with a comb that she never failed in putting her aunt to sleep during their special grooming ritual. A full-grown Shirley finally asked the question that got the Mother of the Movement to reveal a version of that historic December 1, 1955, day not quite like any that has been documented since.

We were taught a bit about the civil rights movement in school, but a lot of it was glossed over. My teachers in the late 1960s actually told us the movement only made things worse for the people who participated. A lot of these battles were still taking place when I was growing up, and uprisings were happening in northern cities, too. Maybe the teachers wanted to keep us from becoming rebellious, because I was taught that all Rosa Parks did was sit down on the bus, like it was a simplistic gesture with no connection to change. I would go to class never identifying myself as her sixth niece, but these "lessons" always bothered me, because Auntie Rosa didn't seem like the kind of person who committed simpleminded acts.

Over twenty years later, sometime in the early 1990s, I talked with her about that day. I said, "Auntie Rosa, I've done a little bit of reading about our history: People were sprayed with fire hoses.

People were beaten. People were taken out into the woods and never found again. What really happened with you?" After she'd been quiet about it for so long, I was about to hear firsthand the story that forever changed her life.

She explained that, under the Jim Crow laws, white and "colored" people were segregated in every aspect of life. In bus segregation, when both the "white" section and "colored" section were filled, a black person had to stand and give up his or her seat to the next white passenger who boarded. Auntie Rosa had had run-ins before with the man who drove her bus that day. She had caught his eye from doing her work with the NAACP, possibly in the neighborhood, or mingling with fellow activists when she was helping register black people to vote, and the driver resented her for that. If you were "colored," you had to pay your fare at the front of the bus, get back off, and enter through the rear door to get to your seat—or stand if the bus was full. Sometimes the driver would let Auntie Rosa pay her fare and wait for her to get off; then he would leave before she could get on again. She was able to make it onto the bus this day, obviously.

"I sat in the first seat for *colored* people," Auntie Rosa told me, "and a white man got on the bus. Mind you, there were very few white people, so their section wasn't full, but he sat in the last seat for whites."

I know a lot of stories that have been written tell you the bus was crowded that day, but that wasn't the reason Auntie Rosa was told to get up. According to the Jim Crow laws, if there weren't many people on the bus, there should be some separation between the end of the "white" rows and the beginning of the "colored" rows so they weren't directly next to each other. The man who sat in the last "white" row that day did it so Auntie Rosa and the other black passengers would be forced to move back.

The white man "laughed when the bus driver told all the black people to get up, which they did, except for me," Auntie Rosa said.

"Weren't you afraid of being hurt?" I asked.

"No, even though a woman was dragged off the bus and beaten and taken to jail a few days earlier. When the policemen came, they escorted me off the bus. They were very nice to me. They even gave me water at the jail."

Nice?

Now, *that* wasn't a word I expected to hear!

I was reminded of Shadrach, Meshach, and Abednego from the Book of Daniel, who were thrown into the fiery furnace and came out unharmed. God put a hedge around Auntie Rosa that day, and she came out of her furnace, not only free of burns, but with a drink to cool off!

"Why didn't you set the facts straight?" I asked her. Auntie Rosa explained that she had tried, but the media didn't report it all correctly. The part about her arrest was sensationalized into a story that grew wings and took off. But she was never the type of person to run toward a camera. We talked at length that day and, as I was leaving, I gave her a portrait I had painted of her. She was grateful. Before we parted, I asked Auntie Rosa one final question: "What do you think is your legacy, and what do you want for the future?"

Auntie Rosa described a world in which people acted without hesitating whenever and wherever they identified a true need. The lady who became known for sitting down told me she wanted us to stand up! From then on, I looked at Auntie Rosa in a different light. She never had talked much, but when she did, her words were filled with wisdom. She felt like she was part of the solution. Not *the* solution, but part of the solution. When the goal was ending legal discrimination, she made a major contribution to that. She made a contribution of a different kind to our family. We would forever know that we shared the same blood as a woman of great pride, courage, and character.

—SHIRLEY

Our Family's Affair

In 1957, Auntie Rosa, Uncle Parks, and our grandmother arrived at our home on Deacon Street in Detroit. When we saw our father, aunt, and grandmother together, we couldn't help but notice how much they resembled one another. They smiled, hugged, and cried upon their initial greeting. We didn't find out until years later why this particular day was so emotional: our grandmother and Auntie Rosa hadn't seen our father in years, since after he'd served in World War II. After reaching Michigan, he vowed never to return to the South because of the ongoing mistreatment of people of color, and he never did.

Our parents met at a restaurant in South Carolina when Father—we didn't call him "Daddy" or "Dad"—was home on leave from the military. They were married soon after. Once Father was honorably discharged, he went back to Alabama for a short time, and soon they began a family. In search of better lives for all of us, they made the trek north to find work and decided to leave the oldest children, Mary and Sylvester Jr., with our grandmother; Auntie Rosa; and her husband, Uncle Parks, who could take care of them until our parents found a new home. After Father secured a job at Chrysler in Detroit, our mother returned to Alabama to retrieve her children, but by this time, a bond had formed between Auntie Rosa and the two oldest children. Auntie Rosa and Uncle Parks provided for Sylvester Jr. and Mary from the time they were infants until their toddler years, so it was tough, at first, for the adults and children to separate. Fortunately, all this was resolved by the time everyone met again on Deacon Street. Father had urged Auntie Rosa, Uncle Parks, and Grandma to come north for quite some time. Looking back, and knowing how Auntie Rosa felt about handling her own responsibilities, they probably hesitated to leave Alabama because they valued their independence, and our parents were the closest family they had in Michigan. She and Uncle Parks were in no position to immediately uproot and settle into a new house of their own. Plus, they knew space was limited and there were now many more mouths to feed at the McCauley residence; in Montgomery, it was just them and Grandma. But back then, it was a lot more common for multiple families to save money and share the workload under one roof like they decided to do. It was a great reunion, with the understanding that we would have five adults and nine children crammed into a three-bedroom, one-bathroom house. While filled to capacity, it still provided shelter for us and a safe haven for our dear relatives.

"There's always room for family," is what Father said.

Auntie Rosa's husband, Raymond, who she called "Parks," was a barber. He would get up in the morning and walk down the street to the shop where he rented a chair. It had an old-fashioned barber's pole in front, with red and white stripes. Uncle Parks was pleasant and playful in nature. He told us jokes, and whatever he did for one of us, he did for all of us; he didn't show favoritism among the children. Uncle Parks was the brother our father never had.

Sundays were bustling at our house. Grandmother and Auntie Rosa would help our mother clean and prepare Sunday supper, with Grandmother and Auntie Rosa doing all the cooking while Mother relaxed. Father would go to Eastern Market to buy the chickens that would often become our main meal of chicken and dumplings. In our backyard, he'd twist the necks off the chickens and they ran around, headless, with us kids running and screaming in the background. Our father performed this task just as naturally as taking a breath.

Auntie Rosa was a true Southern cook. She often treated us with homemade chicken and dumplings, collard greens, ham and cabbage, or salmon croquettes. Here are recipes for some of the favorites we enjoyed during Sunday dinners at Auntie Rosa's house.

CORNBREAD SILVER DOLLAR GRIDDLE CAKES

Auntie's griddle cakes never changed in size nor flavor over the years.

1 cup yellow cornmeal
1 cup flour
1 teaspoon salt
¼ cup sugar
2 teaspoons baking powder
1 egg
1 cup buttermilk
¼ cup vegetable oil

Sift together yellow cornmeal, flour, salt, sugar, and baking powder. Add egg, buttermilk, and vegetable oil, and stir to combine.

Heat a cast-iron griddle to medium heat.

Using a tablespoon, spoon batter onto the hot griddle to about the size of silver dollars. Cook for a few minutes until bubbles start to form, flip over the griddle cakes, and cook a few more minutes before removing to a plate.

CHICKEN AND DUMPLINGS

1 large onion, chopped

3 stalks celery, chopped

1 tablespoon minced garlic

3 tablespoons butter

1 (2- or 3-lb.) chicken, cut into 8 pieces

Water, to cover

4 bouillon cubes

About 2 cups flour

1 teaspoon salt

Ice water

2 or 3 tablespoons cornstarch

Salt

Pepper

In a large skillet over medium heat, sauté onion, celery, and garlic in butter. Add chicken, water, and bouillon cubes. Reduce heat to medium, and cook for 1 hour. Remove from heat, and let cool.

Meanwhile, prepare dumplings. In a large bowl, combine flour and 1 teaspoon salt. Make a well in the middle of the flour mixture, gradually add ice water, and stir, working from the inside out until a ball of dough forms. (Auntie Rosa wouldn't use a bowl; she used the same board she rolled the dough on, and would place the flour and salt mixture down, make a well in the center, add water, and mix with her fingers until a ball formed.) Set dough aside to rest.

Remove skin and chicken from the bones.

Thicken liquid in the pot with cornstarch, and return chicken to the pot. Season with salt and pepper. Set over medium heat, and bring to a simmer. Do not let liquid thicken too much.

Dust your counter or work surface with a little flour, and roll out dough to ⅛ inch thick. Cut into ½-inch-wide strips, pinch off 1-inch pieces from each strip, and add to the hot liquid. Do not stir. Do this as quickly as possible. Dumplings are done when they float to the top of the pot.

# SUCCOTASH

Our great-great-grandfather Anderson McCauley was Cherokee, and this was a dish that was passed down through several generations of his family.

Onions, chopped
Garlic, chopped
4 cups freshly cut corn
2 cups lima beans
3 teaspoons butter
Salt
Pepper
1 smoked ham hock

In a large soup pot over medium heat, combine onions, garlic, corn, lima beans, butter, salt, pepper, and ham hock. Add water to cover, and cook for 1 hour or until lima beans are tender.

 AUNTIE ROSA'S LEMONADE

Auntie Rosa's lemonade took about a half hour to make because she prepared the lemons, boiling them first, then straining them by hand, always doing everything with patience and love.

Lemons (any quantity you desire)
Sugar to taste

Cut lemons, place in a saucepan, cover with water, and set over medium-high heat. Bring to boil, and boil until lemons break down, rind, oil, and all. (This makes the lemon flavor stronger and more concentrated.) Strain out the lemon pieces, add water and sugar, to taste, to the lemon juice, and serve over ice.

FRUIT COMPOTE

*According to our sister Deb, this treat was always worth
the wait!*

1 large glass jar with a lid (this is what our aunt used
to layer the fruit)

1 cup pineapple chunks
4 tablespoons brandy
1 cup maraschino cherries, with liquid
1 cup sugar
1 cup sliced peaches, sprinkled with honey or brown
sugar

In a large glass jar with a lid, combine pineapple
chunks and 2 tablespoons brandy. Place in the refrigerator and stir, once daily, for 2 weeks. After 2 weeks,
add maraschino cherries and liquid, sugar, and remaining 2 tablespoons brandy. Return the jar to the
refrigerator and stir, once daily, for 2 more weeks.
Add peaches, and return to the refrigerator for 2 final
weeks.

Serve fruit over a scoop of vanilla ice cream or a
slice of pound cake.

Auntie Rosa was laid-back and had a great sense of humor, and with her slight Southern accent, she always got our attention when clever things came out of her mouth. But there was one topic that she didn't discuss a lot or joke about. She and Uncle Parks couldn't have children, so we quickly became the sons and daughters she never got the chance to raise. Once, Auntie Rosa was overheard saying, "Brother has all these children, and I don't have any." She would have loved to bring her own sons or daughters into the world, but it must not have been God's plan. In the end, she would have thirteen of us, plus more people around the world, who called her "mother" than many biological moms put together.

Beautiful Auntie Rosa taking her hair down before turning in for the night (1986)

Her long hair was usually pinned up tightly, but when she let it down, it hung past her back, almost behind her knees. Sometimes she'd let the girls comb it—a ritual that would be repeated for years to come, even by the next generation of grand-nieces who also loved and adored her.

We enjoyed it when Auntie Rosa told us stories about her childhood with "Brother"—she didn't call our father "Sylvester"—and how she had to keep him out of trouble as a boy. He was full of mischief, and sometimes Auntie Rosa would hide him from Grandma when she wanted to spank him. Auntie Rosa saw herself as his protector, and she had her work cut out for her: she hid Father well and often. Time passed, and Auntie Rosa found work as a seamstress, something she enjoyed and had done in Alabama. Sewing was a skill she learned from Grandma. She even taught an adult vocational class on the subject for Detroit Public Schools in 1965. Detroit really wrapped its arms around her, and once, when she and Uncle Parks were struggling, a tribute dinner was held for her at Cobo Hall. Coretta Scott King and Ralph Abernathy were the speakers, and fliers advertised ten-dollar donations with "proceeds going to Mrs. Parks." It was only nine years after the end of the bus boycott, and she was still in the process of becoming stable again, so every little bit helped.

After a few months, Auntie Rosa and Uncle Parks were able to rent their own flat on Detroit's east side, and Grandma moved in with them, so our home was a little less crowded. In 1965, Auntie Rosa took a job in the office of Congressman John Conyers, and some years later she started working on her vision for a youth

Our parents purchased this house in Detroit, Michigan, in 1950. Auntie Rosa, Uncle Parks, and Grand- mother lived here after their exodus from the South.

nonprofit agency, the Rosa and Raymond Parks Institute for Self Development. She would occasionally make public appearances around this time. She was a beloved citizen in her community and around the country. The nation had changed, including much of the South, and her face was recognized by people who always wanted to touch her or shake her hand. Though Auntie Rosa still made time to show up at our birthday parties, holidays, and re- unions, she mainly kept her family life private. A few exceptions were when she invited us to the NAACP dinners where she was a regular guest.

In 1977, when both Uncle Parks and our father died only a few months apart, Auntie Rosa became an emotional anchor for our family. She didn't even show signs of breaking down after losing the two most important men in her life. Now, she had thirteen nieces and nephews. Only four short years later, our mother joined Father and Uncle Parks. Who could we look to for guidance? The support Auntie Rosa showed each of us in different ways is what nurtured us through the various stages of our adulthood and soon helped us teach our own children the values she exemplified.

—DEBORAH, ROSALIND, RHEA, SUSAN, AND SHEILA

Anniversary celebration with the entire family at Daisy and Sylvester McCauley's house in Detroit, Michigan (1972)

Home Away from Home

Auntie Rosa's move out of our house into her new place with Uncle Parks was an interesting transition. With so many bodies all under one roof on South Deacon Street, virtually anything could be happening in our home at any given time. There would be a philosophical discussion in one room, somebody might be drawing artwork in another part of the house, and another couple of siblings might be arguing elsewhere. All the while, my father would be either reading the newspaper or watching television, pretty much ignoring everything else around him. He worked hard at Chrysler, full time, and then he also did carpentry or handyman jobs on the weekends, rising before the sun a lot of days and not resting until dark; toiling from "can't see to can't see," as he called it. So in those rare moments that he found to take an opportunity to check out the day's news or peek at an old movie, it wasn't hard for him to drown out everything else. I guess my father created his own version of "quiet time."

Once Auntie Rosa and Uncle Parks settled into their new place with Grandma, it felt like something was missing. Even though they were still a whole lot closer to us than they had been while living in Alabama, a part of the atmosphere that we now associated with home traveled with them to a different address. I found myself often wanting to go to their house. It was tidy, and the smell of Grandma's buttermilk pancakes and cornbread permeated the air. Sometimes when I went to visit, after all the chores were finished, she and I would stay up late, eating cornbread soaked in buttermilk, or graham crackers with peanut butter, along with a glass of cold milk. Despite my feeling that my own mother was the best cook in the world, the thought of Grandma's pancakes, oatmeal, and stewed prunes drew me like nothing else.

Visiting Auntie Rosa's new address was like a trip to the library. I immersed myself in reading material that dealt with racial issues. At a young age, I really wanted to find out why people like me, Auntie Rosa, and our family were considered so different that there had ever been separate places for us to sit on a bus, or separate bathrooms to use at the same highway stops. Sometimes I would get so absorbed in Auntie Rosa's literature that Grandma felt the need to interrupt me now and then.

"Chee-Chee," she'd say, "get your head out of that book and go outside to get some fresh air."

I'd do as I was told for as short a time as I could get away with, come back in and finish a chore, then quickly search out another book. Now and then, history even came to life when I was visiting with Auntie Rosa and my grandmother: I read Lerone Bennett Jr.'s 1962 book, *Before the Mayflower*, and had the opportunity to meet him.

"Be on your best behavior," Auntie Rosa reminded me after saying that the author was coming to her house. I was so excited! We were all taught social graces so we could present ourselves properly whenever Auntie Rosa introduced us to special guests. I made the bad call of deciding to show off my curtsy for classmates at school. It was a skill I learned at some point while visiting my aunt, in between dates when she hosted acquaintances. When I demonstrated the gesture for the other children, they all fell out laughing. That was the last time I would ever waste my social graces on them! But I did my best to be graceful when Mamie Till Bradley visited Auntie Rosa. She was the mother of Emmett Till, whose brutal killing in 1955, just a few months before my aunt was arrested, was a flashpoint for the civil rights movement. Mrs. Till was sweet, soft-spoken, and reminded me of a doll; I remember that she liked me. Meeting her and hearing the story of her son's death made me question our nation's true level of commitment to preserving human rights. Looking at her right there in my aunt's living room was more evidence than I had ever read in any of Auntie Rosa's books that America had two different standards of justice.

Auntie Rosa continued to lead a fairly quiet, normal life; by no means was she a magnet for attention or a media target the way she had been during her final years in Alabama. But her new home seemed to bustle with people and activity. If someone connected to the ongoing battle for equality was in town, like Mrs. Till had been, Auntie Rosa was happy to entertain. It was clearly a part of who she was as a person to want to see wrongs turned into righteousness and to identify with those who were addressing the wrongs. Once, in an interview with Judith Martin, the journalist who went on to write those "Miss Manners" columns, Auntie Rosa made the simple statement, "It seems to me it's natural to want to be treated as a human being." Since she held this attitude, I suppose it felt natural for her to open her home to others, known and unknown, who shared her point of view.

I tried as hard as I could to keep up with the activities and guest appearances at my new home away from home, perfecting the art of appreciating more mature ideas and accomplishing personal tasks far beyond my years. It wasn't all just current events and national affairs, either. Auntie Rosa taught me advanced sewing techniques—turning pockets or making aprons, heating pads, and hand puppets. This nurtured my creative side, as I would later become an artist, like my older brother, Asheber, and my younger sister, Shirley. Without ever intending it to be, Aun-

Left to right: Rhea McCauley, Auntie Rosa, Renee Fussello (Rhea's daughter)

tie Rosa had established for me a training ground for discovering my place in the world. A classroom, visitors bureau, and crafts shop all in one. I still carry pride about the experiences I had there and the people I met, realizing I encountered most of them only because they were also proud to be in Auntie Rosa's company. At this special house, her appeal was reflected in ways big and small. A man's home can be his castle, but there, she was truly a queen.

—RHEA

Stronger Than Blood

For some reason, when Father and Auntie Rosa were talking and spending time together, it was like they were in a world by themselves. It was obvious to anyone who knew them that they cared for each other, like so many brothers and sisters typically do. Father was very protective of her and of our grandmother as well. But the connection between him and Auntie Rosa was something that had a meaning only they could truly appreciate. It wasn't the type of thing that excluded others or made the rest of the family feel any less loved by either one of them; it seemed more like a closeness between old friends who also happened to be siblings.

Father's garden stretched across three rented lots where he grew greens, tomatoes, peppers, cucumbers, squash, green beans, and lima beans. We also had apple trees, plum trees, and cherry

Auntie Rosa's father,
James McCauley (1923)

trees that we tended, pulling weeds and breaking clods of dirt. There was even a strawberry patch and an arbor with red and white grapes. This was the tranquil setting where he and our aunt would go off and talk, sometimes for hours, as they strolled the little urban farm. Father would stop now and then, kneeling to check his latest harvest or maybe drizzling the plants with water, as they chatted contently. We were never involved in this one-on-one time, but we imagined them talking about some of the things they had been through together, maybe even going back to their childhood, before any of us had become a thought. Theirs was a bond that went back so many decades, to when they first became a young support team for Grandma after our grandfather left the family.

May 15, 1950.
Patterson Calif

My Dear Daughter

I Received Your letter of May 5th. a few days ago and was indeed Glad to hear from you. and the otheres. that go to make up the family. and to learn that all was Well. and that Sylvester was married and doing Well. was indeed a Pleasure.

Yes I wrote to sister Jessie Bell. at Eufaula Ala. first. she Informed me of Deaths. of Mother. Bro. Robert and George. I also Written to sister Addie at Ozark. and inquired of you. she said you was still in Montgomery but failed to give me your street adress. in her first letter but did so in her second one. I Keept thinking of Writting You. and still putting it off. it was in view of the fact that I was over shadowed. with open shame that I. and I alone allowed the Evil spirit to lead me Completly out of Myself for these many years. in Those desertion of a a good Wife and two of the sweetest Children every I lived. and at a time when I was needed most. I dread to Mention these unpleasant events to you. but as I am now on the sun set side of life. I need to unburden myself of these Sins of such Cruel nature I some time think they are unforgiveable.

Please "You" and Mother forgive me. I will Write Brother Soon.

I am "Glad to say tat this Writting that I am well and am in Very good health I dont Work regular. here in California about 3 years I will be in Modesto After May 20th I have some work their.

I will appreciate the Pictures if you will send them to General Delivery Modesto Calif.

Give My best Regards to Mother and Parks. James

May 15, 1950

Parterson, Calif

My Dear Daughter,

    I received your letter of May 5th, a few days ago and was indeed glad to hear from you and the others that go to make up the family, and to learn that all was well and that Sylvester was married and doing well was indeed a pleasure.

    Yes I wrote to sister Jessie Bell at Eufala, Ala. first she informed me of deaths of mother bro Robert and George. I've written to sister Addie at Ozark and inquired of you. She said you was still in Montgomery but failed to give me your street address in her first letter but did so in her second one. I kept thinking of writting [writing] *you and still putting it off. It was in view of the fact that I was overshadowed with open shame that I and I alone allowed the evil spirit to lead me completely out of myself for these many years in grose* [gross] *desertion of a good wife and two of the sweetest children ever lived. And at a time when I was needed most. I dread to mention these unpleasent events to you but as I am now on the sunset side of life, I need to unburden myself of these sins of such cruel nature and sometime think they are unforgivable.*

    Please you and mother forgive me; I will write Brother soon. I am glad to say at this writing that I am well and am in very good health I don't work regular here in California about 3 years I will be in Modesto after May 20th. I have some work their [sic]. *I will appreciate the pictures if you will send them to General Delivery Modesto Calif.*

    Give my best regards to mother and Parks. James

WHEN FATHER DIED of stomach cancer in 1977, Auntie Rosa said she would always be grateful to our mother because she was by Father's side every day. We had never seen Auntie Rosa cry until she spoke at his funeral. Auntie Rosa probably never expected "Brother" to be the first of them to die. Some of us were still teenagers, and she seemed to feel responsible for us even more after he was gone. It showed in so many of the ways that she became a bigger presence in our lives. It showed in the manner that she parented us, naturally, without having experienced parenthood for herself at all. Thinking about it now, we realize that nearly thirty years of bonding with Auntie Rosa after her brother passed was an extension of the bond she had first formed with him during their childhood. Her devotion to all of us grew from one of the most important relationships she ever had.

—SHEILA AND RHEA

Heart of a Mother

I was furious with my parents. It was my junior year at one of the best high schools in Detroit. I found myself struggling to keep up academically and at the same time complete my daily house chores. I felt my mother and father were not being supportive enough; instead, they were working against me, making my life tougher. I was usually a rather docile middle child, but on this

Grandfather James McCauley first visited our family in 1961.
Tall and friendly, he had a calm, centered spirit. We believe a lot was
settled between Auntie Rosa, Father, and Grandfather during his visit.
Shortly after returning to California, Grandfather passed away.

From left to right, front to back:
1st row: William, Sheila, Shirley
2nd row: Susan, Rhea, Robert, Deborah
3rd row: Asheber, Mary, Rosalind, Hannah Mae
4th row: Daisy McCauley, Sylvester McCauley Sr., James McCauley

particular afternoon, an overreaction would set my life on a different course. I was certainly tired. I had a ninth-hour class that day, and I caught the city bus home, riding with an armload of books. I looked forward to, at least, two hours of homework that night.

Well, when I walked through the door, I was incensed that my family was impatiently waiting for me to prepare dinner, given that it was my week to cook. The three oldest sisters still living at home would rotate the main chores, and the schedule listed meals as Sue's assignment. I knew my father was hungry after waiting two hours for me to come home, but I'd had a long day. When he told me, "Get the slop on," I did something nobody, including me, expected: I exploded.

"Get your own damn slop!" I yelled, running upstairs to my room in tears. I had never raised my voice, much less uttered a profane word, to my parents. The stress of a challenging semester and frustration from what I saw as a lack of understanding all came spilling out of me in just those few seconds. My father called after me, angrily, but I didn't answer. Through my tears and hurt, I decided that if my parents didn't care to support me, I didn't care anymore, either. Why try so hard just to be shot down?

I MADE GOOD on my bad decision: senior year for me was all partying and fun. Where I'd carried home, literally, pounds' worth of books the previous semesters, now I barely studied at all.

I did just enough to get by. My once-coveted grade point average plummeted. I don't know how I thought I'd get into college. I didn't even study for my entrance exams, staying out late to party with friends the night before. As a result, my scores were border-line for admission. I barely qualified to get into any college, much less the ones I wanted to attend. My grade point average was so low, in fact, that I had to find a program I could begin during the summer, taking remedial courses to prepare me for what lay ahead in my freshman year. With reality setting in, I jumped at the op-portunity.

I soon found myself in a wonderful dormitory on a beautiful college campus in a suburban setting. Oakland University was less than an hour from home, in Rochester. I was off to a practi-cally brand-new start. What more could a girl ask for? It wasn't too long before I found my answer: trouble. I had barely gotten settled into the dorm, and classes hadn't even started, so I was bored. I decided to go exploring with a dorm mate. We had only ventured as far as the lobby when a security officer demanded to see my student ID card. I had neglected to carry it with me, and the officer didn't hesitate to let me know I was in violation of "ordinance" this and "code" that. What was going on? Next, he grabbed my arm to escort me out—I snatched away. Well, why did I do that? Now, not only did he cite me with a violation, but the university wasted no time banning me from living in the dor-mitories. So much for my brand-new start after high school.

I didn't have a car. How could I go to class if I couldn't live on campus anymore? I called my mother in tears, needing advice on what direction to take. The only thing I knew for sure was that I wasn't going back home. What happened after I hung up with my mother, I never found out, but the next call I got was from Auntie Rosa. She had a friend who happened to live in a town nearby, and her friend was willing to rent me a room for the rest of the quarter. I couldn't believe I was getting this blessing! Almost as quickly as my world started falling apart, my aunt was working behind the scenes to help me pull the pieces back together. I would miss out on the convenience and experience of living on campus for a while, but that was a minor setback compared with the thought of sitting out the whole term I'd prepared for.

Auntie Rosa never even questioned me about what led to my getting into so much trouble. She knew how important the opportunity to go to college was, and she didn't want me to lose that opportunity. Period. Especially over something that seemed so trivial, it would have felt devastating, but she didn't bother to find out what the trivial incident was. Looking back, now with children of my own, I realize Auntie Rosa had the heart of a mother. A mother believes in the goodness and potential of her child and is willing to defend that child with her own life. Auntie Rosa felt she knew my character well enough to extend herself on my behalf, refusing to let whatever error in judgment I might have made determine my future. The help she gave let me stay on track without having to start that tough journey I had walked all over again. This was one of several times that she inspired me to not only get up when I fell down, but to get up and run faster!

A FEW YEARS after that rocky start, I had a degree in art from Michigan State University. Even more than the certificate, I had the knowledge that a support system, including parents I once doubted, was always behind me. Having Auntie Rosa in my corner sure didn't hurt, either. The soft heart of a mother can be a rock-solid foundation.

—SUSAN

Team Player

I was my parents' seventh child. While seven is said to be a lucky number, out of my dozen sisters and brothers, I seem to have had the most unlucky of starts. It's said that few of us can truly recall our early years, but I still remember this moment in 1956 as if it were yesterday. I was three and sitting on the sidewalk in front of our house when, suddenly, I realized there was no motor function in my legs. Mary, my older sister, saw me not moving and came over, tugging at my arm.

"Ma!" I remember her saying. "Robert is acting like he can't get up." I tried, with the few words I could use, to explain to her that my legs had no feeling. When she went inside to get my mother, they both found that I was completely paralyzed from the waist down. When I reached Columbia Medical, the doctors examined me. They came back out and told my parents I had contracted polio, but it was treatable. A vaccine was administered, and the doctors gave me a spinal tap. My parents were told to give me plenty of hot baths and to make sure I rested. I had only just learned to walk; now it would be a few weeks before I took steps on my own again. With all of my brothers and sisters, I had plenty of company, even though I couldn't play with them the way I had become accustomed. By the time Auntie Rosa moved to Detroit the following year, I was on my feet again. It was our first-ever meeting, and I would grow to love her for the rest of my life. She became a great example of how I could take a stand in ways that had nothing to do with my legs.

My early encounters with Auntie Rosa usually took place at the dinner table with all my siblings and I joining one another for meals. At that time, we were really glad to have food. There was a point after Auntie Rosa arrived when my father's fellow Chrysler workers decided to go on strike. This left him temporarily jobless, challenged with finding ways to keep on filling what must have seemed like an endless line of empty plates. Our family grew to be quite large, even compared with what was thought of as big families back then. There was a different standard from today in the way households functioned, and women didn't take birth control pills. Abortion was illegal, and it was generally thought of as immoral, too. Most of the time, your home grew to be whatever size it was when you stopped having children, and that was that. You were expected to do what it took to care for them, and my father, Sylvester, provided for us the best way he could. But it was a good thing to have Auntie Rosa there as well, sometimes giving her many nephews and nieces the greatest gift of all—something to eat! To this day, I'm still fond of organizations like the Salvation Army and Goodfellows charities, because without them, there would have been a lot of Christmases for us without any other kind of gifts. There were occasions when these organizations also helped put clothes on my back.

Through Auntie Rosa then, and watching her in the years to come, I learned that time and commitment were also gifts one can give to others. I think that, to a large degree, society today has gone astray because we've gotten so far away from understanding that. If more of us had less to give that was of material value, as was the case with my aunt and her generation so long ago, I think we would have learned the principles that she held on to and carried with her out into the world. Having such a giving person in my family always made it easy for me to want to give back to her when I saw opportunities.

Around the time my aunt was still blending with our family, I got an important assignment from my father. He taught me and some of my siblings how to till the soil and make things grow. Because it wasn't only me who learned, I sometimes came to resent the task of caring for our family's garden. Weeding. Planting. Cultivating. At eight years old, it sometimes felt like I was doing all the work. Still, there was a bonus result: I could be proud that I was instrumental in growing food Auntie Rosa herself sometimes prepared on her stove. I never felt like a freeloader on those days when we went to her house to get a square meal.

She always welcomed all of us into her home. Even though

there were mischief-driven times when one of my brothers and I would find Uncle Parks' discarded cigarette butts and go hide so we could smoke them, I really grew to respect Auntie Rosa's husband. Throughout their decades of marriage, he was content to let her have recognition and shine as a public figure. Not every man's ego can handle living with a woman who's more prominent in the community than he is, but he was happy to stand in the background. That's a lot of love.

In a way, what Uncle Parks did for her was the same thing she had done for Martin Luther King. Auntie Rosa became secretary of Montgomery's NAACP in 1943, at age twenty, and she was promoted to Alabama's state secretary by 1948. This was a big deal and an important position in those days. Remember, there would be a major movement brewing across the South in the next several years, and being the officer of an organization that was at the forefront made my aunt's rank and input key.

Contrary to what a lot of the public still believes, she wasn't just a woman who casually decided she was going to jail in 1955. She was well connected and schooled in protest. It wasn't a coincidence that Dr. King, who was from Georgia and had only started preaching in Montgomery a year earlier, became the head of a boycott sparked by Auntie Rosa's arrest. He was known to the community, but he needed people like her to build the movement in Alabama. It's interesting to imagine that King himself might not have become as known to the world if not for my aunt's actions in the city of Montgomery. Think of it: if she had never put her own freedom on the line then, today we might not have a national holiday honoring a black man who battled for freedom. Knowing how to step up, like she did to help our family, and how to step back at the appropriate time, like she did when Dr. King took over the movement, made Auntie an asset to every team she joined.

—ROBERT

Her Quiet Companion

It's strange to think that Auntie Rosa became so well-known around the world in part due to her gentle, quiet personality. It seemed that people were drawn to her even more because she wasn't this fiery woman who demanded attention when she was around a crowd, not even when the crowd was gathered because of her. She was truly the same person whether you saw her on-stage at a big public event or sitting at home in her living room. Calm and reserved as she had always been, Uncle Parks was her true equal. Maybe opposites do attract, but the fellow who gave Auntie Rosa his last name had a personality that was a lot like hers.

Uncle Parks was a sweet man and not very talkative. The most we usually heard out of him was during those in-depth conversations the adults would have about things happening out in the world. Maybe that was to be expected from people who had been affected by large-scale conflicts their whole lives: Auntie Rosa getting arrested was because of the politics that created segregation laws; Father had gone to war where he followed orders from the government regarding America's enemies; and Uncle Parks had been an activist all the way back into the 1930s, working to help the Scottsboro Boys, nine Alabama teenagers whose cases went all the way to the Supreme Court when they were falsely accused of rape. Like our aunt's, Uncle Parks' passion for justice must have burned from the inside, because we never heard him shout. It was still a time of debating issues, and there was a lot of community organizing taking place, so there were plenty of past and current events for him and the other adults to weigh in on.

He was a genuine creature of habit. At work in the barbershop, he had a small stool he'd sit on all day, cutting hair until evening. He'd come back home, get supper, and then sit down in his favorite chair. Auntie Rosa took care of Uncle Parks if he was sick and made sure he had food to eat, but they weren't what you'd call an affectionate couple. Along with our grandmother, they just had this comfortable Southern dynamic in their own home, and they were always together. As a matter of fact, the only time we ever saw Uncle Parks upset was when our aunt wasn't around. She'd go away for an engagement, and sometimes our grandmother, who was a pistol, would irritate him. They'd fuss and he would say, "I'll be glad when Rosa gets back!" A lot of times, he started missing Auntie before she even left the house.

He felt as close to us as a blood relative, which didn't change after he and our aunt moved out to their own home. Uncle Parks didn't have a car, so he'd ride the bus to our place just to take us out for ice cream or walk us to the park. Even though he wasn't a forceful person, he had a spirit that we missed once he was gone, nobody more so than our aunt. She loved him and made certain his name was remembered right beside hers when she opened the Rosa and Raymond Parks Institute years after he died. It doesn't always take a loud voice to get the attention you deserve.

—DEBORAH, ROSALIND, AND SHEILA

Service for a Smile

My brothers and sisters had pretty much turned into office people. I was the youngest, and I took after my father. Out of all those hands in our family, mine stayed the dirtiest. Fixing and building were natural things for me. As a kid with a paper route, it was hard work delivering to three hundred houses, on foot, and then having to get ready for school. After wearing out my sneaker soles for so long, I came up with a new approach. I'd have to be careful, though, because you were talked about back then if you got caught going through garbage in the neighborhood. And I didn't want to get talked about.

Now, they give you a license to go around picking up things people throw out, which is hard for me to believe, but in those days, people put all kinds of things they didn't want out at the curb. So that's where I started my treasure hunt. I'd go from house to house, looking over my shoulders to make sure none of my friends saw me, and then pick up anything I could use. One part, then another part. After searching for weeks, I had tires and handlebars, and I found a seat. In a while, I had built my own bike, and I didn't have to walk my paper route anymore.

So, that was my thing. Fixing stuff. By the time I got to be around eighteen or nineteen, I had graduated to electronics. On trips with my father to Auntie Rosa's house, I kept seeing this old RCA shortwave radio, but she never listened to it. It was made in 1931 or '32, and it was big, like eighteen to twenty inches tall and fourteen inches wide, with just one speaker and four knobs in front. It would just sit there in her living room like a piece of furniture, but she was moving it, along with other things, because she was getting a new place. She told me it didn't work, but if I could fix it, I could have it.

So I took it home with me and started taking it apart. While I was working on the radio, I found out the history behind it: it was a wedding present from her husband. He had given it to her when they were still living in Alabama. I guess she kept it to remind her of him after he died. Maybe they thought one day they would get it working and use it again when Uncle Parks was still around, but that never happened. Well, the more I heard and learned about the significance of it, the more my plan changed. I decided I would refurbish it for her and give it back so she could enjoy it again, but she didn't know that. There was just one problem—that was back when TVs and radios took tubes, and tubes were expensive. I couldn't fix it without that particular part. I only knew one way to come up with the money, since I wasn't on anybody's regular payroll. To finish this fix-it job I had to find more fix-it jobs.

As you'd probably guess, it took me some time to do all that side work and then buy the tube. Finding the part, now that I was able to pay for it, turned out to be the hardest part of all. They were almost obsolete for that model, RCA Victor, but finally, I found one and got the radio working again. Then I bought the equipment to finish the wooden cabinets. I did all this by myself. I'll never forget that moment when I went to see her and put the radio in Auntie Rosa's hands. She was excited about it. She had probably thought she'd never switch that RCA on again. Well, pretty soon she was listening to her news programs and talk radio. She never watched a lot of TV. The radio was made before you had AM and FM; you had long wave and short wave. On the long wave, you could pick up overseas stations, but Auntie Rosa tuned it to local shows, like Martha Jean "The Queen," who was real popular. She did a lot of comment and community news. During the '67 rebellion in Detroit, when buildings all over the city were burning, she stayed on the air for forty-eight hours straight, trying to calm things down and telling people to stay inside rather than go out to loot or get caught in police sweeps. It was the early '80s now, but she still had a lot of faithful listeners. And Auntie Rosa could follow what was going on from "The Queen's" perspective, or anybody else's whenever she turned that old RCA's dial. She liked to keep up on as much information as she could, so she used to listen to it religiously.

Not too long after that, I got a job in New Jersey and moved out there where my sister, Sheila, was living. I didn't move back to Detroit for years and, for some reason, I didn't see that radio around again. Nobody in the family could tell me where it was, either. I learned that Auntie Rosa had planned on leaving me the RCA after she died, but now Auntie Rosa was getting sick and she was having dementia. Later on, I found out it was donated to one of the Rosa Parks historical collections. I don't even know if she knew that happened. From what I understand, it still works.

I'm disappointed that I never got it back, the one material thing I know meant a lot to my aunt. It would have been a nice way to remember her, the same way she kept it to remember Uncle Parks. But even if I don't have it, I still have the memory of that day when I gave it to her, working like it was brand new. Right now I can close my eyes and see the way she smiled. That moment, in my mind, can never be taken away from me.

—RICHARD

A Gift of Greatness

She wasn't the type of person who got easily offended. Most of us can't even remember a single time when she raised her voice. But there was one thing I used to say, now and then, that seemed to bother Auntie Rosa. She'd always correct me when she heard me say a particular word: *great*.

"I'm just your auntie," she'd say. "Don't call me your *great-auntie*." The issue had nothing to do with vanity or shame about her increasing age. Auntie Rosa wanted us to feel close to her and to understand that the chronological distance and years between our generations made us no less her family. Whether it was the dinners at Cobo Hall, where she'd invited us during my childhood, or the many holiday gatherings she hosted at her home, Auntie

Rosa's message was always the same. Spoken or unspoken, it was understood that we were all important to her. No matter how far she traveled, how long she was gone, or what important things she was doing, our place deep in her heart didn't change.

At those annual Cobo dinners, usually held by the NAACP, I was small, but I knew how to ask crucial questions, such as "What are we having to eat?" Another one, when I'd see her at the head table in those big banquet halls, was, "Why is Auntie Rosa sitting up there?" My parents would shush me at these dinners. I must have been asking at the wrong time. I didn't learn the importance of who Auntie Rosa was in the movement, or why she held a place of honor among the others in the room, until later when I was in school. *Wow! People are singing songs about her*, I remember thinking. At my young age, while sitting before those large, cloth-covered tables, I only knew that I was enjoying dinner out with my family, just like we'd all enjoyed it the year before. Auntie Rosa would have been glad to know I saw it that way. Her presence at these banquets was important to the hosts, but our presence is what was important to her.

My aunt spoke to me frequently about the significance of family. Because I'm the oldest of more than twenty of her grand-nephews and grand-nieces, she probably thought I should hear how meaningful staying connected was, from her perspective. Auntie Rosa knew it would take more than her and my mother, uncles, and aunts to keep the McCauleys united, especially as our family numbers grew. She could be counted on to give her advice to me and my many cousins, just like she had counseled our parents, even if the advice was like the tough love she once gave me when I was dealing with a problem: "You come from better stock. You need to stop being sad and do something about it. Fix it."

She was mentally tough and incredibly smart, so it didn't make the cut with her if we accepted less than our capabilities. High expectations. Pride. Love. These were her gifts to our family. And only one word can describe these gifts: *great*.

—MARC

Nothing to Sweat About

When I was a child, and as I grew up, I used to watch my aunt and grandmother, wondering to myself, *How do they always look so calm and collected?* Of all the photos Auntie Rosa took through the years, including the ones I've seen online and in books, I've never seen a single one that showed her with a hair out of place, never one that showed her disheveled, but always neat and wrinkle-free. There weren't anywhere near as many photos of my grandmother, but she was the same way. She must have been the person Auntie Rosa modeled herself after. As a matter of fact, the older Auntie Rosa got, the more like Grandma she dressed.

Their clothes were almost like uniforms. Even though they dressed in different colors and styles, it was the same articles from top to bottom. Stockings with full undergarments. Sensible shoes. Skirts or dresses made from heavy-looking material. Sometimes a hat. If you saw them out in public a lot, you would have wondered if Auntie Rosa and Grandma could prove they had anything to connect their hands to their necks, because with the long sleeves they always wore, you wouldn't get a glimpse of their arms if you saw them a hundred times. They would stay fully dressed like this until bedtime. It didn't matter if they were only cooking or chatting at the table. Something about the rules of their generations made them feel like they always had to be presentable. Then, if they didn't get right into bed that night, it was always floor-length robes over a gown, with bedroom slippers.

Shorts?

No way.

Sandals?

Forget about it.

Bare feet?

Are you kidding?

I never even saw either of them wear a summer dress!

Once, Auntie Rosa invited all of the family to Boblo Island. Boblo was an amusement park located on some land between Detroit and southwestern Ontario. You had to ride the Boblo boat down the river to get there. It had been around since the late 1890s and lots of families spent summers riding those forty-five minutes up and down the water to and from the island. Well, on the day Auntie Rosa picked out for our family, it was blazing hot outside. The temperature was one hundred degrees, and the sun coming down felt like a gigantic oven, with all of us on the baking rack. People were taking clothes off their children, and a lot of us were so sunburned we could hardly enjoy the games and rides at

Alana (Rosalind Elaine's daughter) with Auntie Rosa on Boblo Island (1991)

the park. Sweat was dripping from everybody's foreheads. And there was Auntie Rosa, smiling, walking around fully dressed in a hat and stockings. She looked as cool as a Popsicle.

After a day of sweating like turkeys near Thanksgiving, we all went back to her house. She was playing her usual great hostess role, asking, "Is everybody okay?" As if she didn't even notice how drained we were from heat exhaustion. We were all looking at one another, amazed. That day always brought us laughs when we remembered it later. We saw her totally composed like this in so many different situations, time after time, no matter what the weather was like.

I know that some might disagree, because a lot of folks have aunts they love, but take my word when I tell you that my auntie was the coolest you've ever seen.

—ROSALIND

Making of a Matriarch

To say there weren't very many women like her doesn't even begin to capture the truth. Obviously, there will only be one Rosa Parks.

To say she was a great example for humanity barely fits the proper description of who she was. The medals and honors she received are strong evidence of that.

To call her one of the most wonderful people I've ever known might still be an understatement. Yet, as the wife of her nephew Asheber, I was fortunate enough to call her "Auntie," too, and she

LEFT: *Rosa Parks' mother, Leona*
RIGHT: *Rosa Parks (née Rosa Louise McCauley) as a baby*

accepted me as family, just as she did our children. My observations of Auntie Rosa and the thirteen men and women who were like her sons and daughters not only increased my respect for her, but also expanded my understanding of what the word *family* truly means.

My daughters are like Auntie Rosa. She had a feisty character, but it was combined with a calming energy, like the ocean waves—soothing to hear, but also unyielding to anything that tries to block their path. Auntie Rosa joined my family for a lot of our outings. She would often drop by the house before running her errands. We'd have our activities, then grab something to eat—and boy, could she ever eat! No one would ever have guessed it just by looking at her.

We had a wonderful relationship, and her company was always a pleasure. She was excited when I got pregnant with the girls, and my interactions with her during that time are some of my favorite memories. I was already joyful about motherhood, and it was a thrill for me to have such a positive and nurturing woman to share in the experience. Auntie Rosa's support and enthusiasm were added benefits, and it was a joy to see that her affection toward children hadn't decreased even slightly now that her nieces and nephews were having families of their own.

When Zakiya was born, Auntie Rosa made sure we got everything we needed. We didn't have a phone, so she bought us one. She also bought baby things to help make her grand-niece's earliest days in the world as comfortable and pleasant as possible.

Auntie Rosa had always been generous, but her kindness at this time was truly overwhelming. She made her love for us obvious by involving herself in whatever ways she could if it fulfilled a need. If she knew there was anything to do, you rarely had to ask.

When my son Malik, Asheber's stepson, turned sixteen, he went through a rites-of-passage program. Just like she was there for so many other big events, she stood front and center as Malik received the praise and encouragement of community leaders like State Representative Ed Vaughn. Elder Vaughn had owned a bookstore and been an activist in Detroit for years.

"Malik, you are my man!" he said. "Make whatever you can come true."

Auntie Rosa urged Malik forward, too.

"Stay strong and don't give up," she said. He did stay strong, and he went on to Morehouse College. He was very proud that day.

Auntie Rosa was always glad to have the whole family visit with her, which wasn't an easy thing because of her large number of nieces and nephews, not including their spouses, like me, and all the children. When our relatives got together, we were content, no matter what the occasion was. She wanted to keep us united, and she didn't like the thought of long time periods passing without seeing us, especially folks who were within driving distance. At the same time, we all knew we had her undivided attention whenever she was available if we needed to go to her and share anything on our minds. Auntie Rosa gladly played the role of counselor and mentor to so many of her loved ones that it would be impossible to repay her for all the time and patience she invested.

She always showed me things that were intangible, those important values you couldn't learn by reading any manual or by sitting in a classroom. Hers was a powerful presence, the kind that penetrates you. In what was just her everyday life, she impacted people without drawing the attention of a boycott or a demonstration, even though we knew she'd been capable of that, too. She was strong, tenacious, and didn't take any *stuff*. You respected Auntie Rosa because she stood up for herself without having to raise her voice or carry on. We continue to carry her spirit and honor her memory.

—NAJMA

Left to right: Najma, Kia, and Auntie Rosa at a family barbeque at Rhea's home in Ypsilanti, Michigan

A Presence Still Felt

Dear Auntie Rosa,

*I want you to know that your spirit is as strong in death
as it was in life. I sense your presence everywhere,
especially within our family, urging us to carry out your
wishes, hopes, and dreams. Urging us to continue your
work. This I promise you: we shall continue your legacy
with the integrity inspired by your spirit. Auntie Rosa, I
remember those brilliant afternoons in Los Angeles,
visiting you at your friends' home. The stream of loving
acquaintances flowed in and out during that visit. I
remember your guest appearance at Rev. Robert Schuller's
Crystal Cathedral in Garden Grove, California. The kids
and I later visited you at the Doubletree Hotel. What I
remember most was your sad smile and you saying you
were tired, so very tired. I wondered why you didn't just
retire then. You weren't ready. You had much more to do.
I yearn for the opportunity to, once again, knock on your
front door and have it open to your smiling face.*

*I remember the notes and cards of encouragement
during my college years; often they were accompanied by
a twenty-dollar bill tucked neatly inside. "Just to help
you out," you would write. I cherish the wonderful people,*

from celebrities to politicians and artists, that I was privileged to meet because they loved you, Auntie. We are all better human beings for sharing the glow of your spirit. May you remain among us forever.

Amen.

—SUSAN

Susan and Auntie Rosa in California

Nov. 28, 1987

To my dear niece
and family:
With love and best
wishes. My prayers
and hope for the
best to all of you
as you renew your
return to new
motherhood with
twin sons,
Aunt Rosa

Feb. 12, 1982

Dear Sheila:

Wishing you a birthday
filled with good times that will last,
Special moments to recall
long after they have passed,
And hoping every single day
throughout the year will bring
Fulfillment joy, and happiness—
the best of everything.

Happy Birthday!
Love always,
Aunt Rosa
P.S. My warm regards to Perry.

Feb. 15, 1989

My dear niece Sheila:

Because you're so nice,
I just couldn't fail
To add my "Hello"
To your Valentine mail!
This is late but sincere
Happy Valentine's Day
I hope you had a
Happy Birthday.
Love to you and family,
Aunt Rosa

Forgiveness

....

We are not in a struggle of black against
white, but wrong and right.

—ROSA PARKS,
March 25, 1965, Montgomery, Alabama

For the woman who came to be regarded as one of the most seminal figures of the civil rights movement, bravery equaled sacrifice. Not only did her resistance bring about a heavy emotional toll, but her newfound infamy made her widely unemployable at only forty-three years old. Forced to start life again in a new city and social climate, she simply regrouped and refocused. Many who suffered such personal loss, without the benefit of support from anyone connected to the movement, might have become deeply embittered. Indeed, as shown throughout history, agents of change have often come to feel that their labors and losses were in vain. As recalled here, however, Mrs. Parks held no resentment in her heart. She always looked forward, even as some who learned of her presence in Michigan openly resented her because of her past.

Mrs. Parks kept her hate mail. Who knows why? Most of her friends and loved ones in Detroit didn't realize she continued receiving it at all. A sampling:

"Why? do you people push yourselves where your [sic] not wanted? . . . much less since those stupid, ignorant colored people act like a bunch of lunatics."

[Dated 1964.]

"We don't think John Conyers should be hiring a person of your low calibre [sic] Rosa, to work in his office. Maybe in his private home for [the] purpose of scrubbing floors as a domestic maid, perhaps— but certainly not doing office work . . . You are far too much of a troublemaker and rabble rouser. We cannot so soon forget all the chaos you made about 'going to the back of the bus.' . . . As a matter of fact, you are to blame[,] gal, for the current revolution going on among the niggers and whites today."

[Dated May 19, 1969.]

Other suggestions included the advice that Mrs. Parks and other "nigs" go "back to Africa." One especially hateful message, dated March 8, 1971, gloated about a news report that she was badly hurt after slipping on ice-covered ground, but it went menacingly further: "By rights[,] you ought to be shot at sunrise, or otherwise appropriately taken care of for your dastardly deed in Montgomery, Alabama . . ."

Could Mrs. Parks have viewed such ink-stained bile as a badge of honor? She is remembered as a "pack rat," but certainly there must have been limits on the mail that she stored. Whatever her reasoning, it speaks even more explicitly to the civil rights champion's refusal to hate those deserving of hatred. Her family shares moving examples of how her forgiving spirit helped shape their views of the world and those who sometimes make it a difficult place in which to live.

Innocence Lost (Part One)

We always went to visit Auntie Rosa, Uncle Parks, and Grandma on Sunday. My father would bring them fruit and vegetables from his garden to last them the entire week. But one Sunday, something was different, and just a few of us rode with Father that day while my mother and most of my brothers and sisters stayed home. Father didn't talk on the drive over and didn't tell us to sit back and be quiet like he usually did. As we drove up to the house, Auntie Rosa, Uncle Parks, Grandma, and some other adults were waiting on the porch. As soon as my father walked up the steps, everyone started to talk at once. I knew something was wrong when my brother, sisters, and I weren't told to go inside or to the backyard to play—the adults in our family never discussed anything important around us. Grandma finally noticed the smaller kids and sent them into the house. I sat quietly off to one side of the porch so I wouldn't be noticed and sent away like the others. Whatever was going on, I wanted to hear about it. With the kids out of sight, or so they thought, the adults began passing around copies of *Jet* and *Look* magazines. From my distance several feet away, I caught a glimpse of a horribly disfigured face; it was the shocking open-casket photo of Emmett Till. I heard them saying that this child, not much older than me, had been murdered, allegedly for whistling at a white woman in Mississippi. He was beaten beyond recognition, weighted down with a heavy cotton gin fan tied around his neck with barbed wire, and thrown into the Tallahatchie River. Everyone was in an uproar.

I listened intently as they discussed black folks who'd gone missing, along with others who were found hanging from trees or floating in rivers like Emmett had been. I suddenly began to realize the risks that my aunt and uncle had taken to stand up against racism, and how brave they truly were. Auntie Rosa had broken the law on a public bus with no one there to protect her; if bigots could drag Emmett out of bed in the middle of the night from a house filled with his family, what might they have done to my aunt with only strangers around?

Just as rage began to rise up inside my nine-year-old body, the conversation ended and the adults tucked away the magazines before going inside. As fate would have it, Auntie Rosa remained on the porch, noticing me for the first time. I went up to her, and all the emotions I felt poured out through tears. "I *hate* white people!" I said, shaking with anger.

Auntie Rosa looked at me tenderly and put her hands on my

shoulders to calm me down. "All white people aren't bad," she said. "Just remember: you are as good as anybody." It was only a few gentle words, but they helped me through that very painful moment. I soon wiped my tears, and we joined the family inside. It impresses me to know that not even the bloody terrorism of Southern hatred in the '50s, terrorism that snatched away children's lives, could harden Auntie Rosa's heart. Yet, I still mourn for Emmett Till, a boy who went to Mississippi to visit relatives, never to return, simply because of the color of his skin.

The color of *my* skin.

—DEBORAH

A Time for Healing

None of us ever saw it coming.

Uncle Parks, who'd been a traditional, protective husband, and had kept a gun at home, was now long gone.

Auntie Rosa was a widow the entire time that she lived in this house on the street called Wildemere where the unthinkable happened during late summer 1994. Pronounced *will-duh-meer*, *Wild*-emere was more like it in our minds after first hearing that our aunt was physically attacked.

It actually wasn't even the most terrible neighborhood. There were much better around Detroit, but there were much worse, too. Typically, Auntie Rosa showed no fear of her surroundings. She was still pretty independent at eighty-one years old, and she'd walk everywhere. Once, one of us drove all the way to Wilde-mere to take her to the post office after she mentioned needing to go. When she was asked, "You ready, Auntie Rosa?" things got more clear: she put on her black, soft-soled walking shoes and started leading the way.

Now, there would be no more strolling the neighborhood. A twenty-something-year-old drug addict had broken in on her, robbed her of fifty-three dollars, and hit her in the face. We were deeply saddened, and some of us were more furious than anything else, but we were also thankful she was alive. There was all kinds of media attention, headlines like "Assailant recognized Rosa Parks." The subtitle for a Pennsylvania story printed in the *Reading Eagle* newspaper was, "A police investigator says that Joseph Skipper was unaware he was breaking into her home, but when he confirmed her identity, he beat her anyway."

It was so hurtful to learn the details: Auntie Rosa told us she found him already inside the house and he asked her for money; when she turned to get a few dollars from her purse, she looked back around and felt the hard blow.

"That was the worst pain I ever felt in my life," Auntie Rosa told us.

"Now gimme some more!" he shouted.

The next day, when she was out of the hospital, we all went to check on her at different times. She would actually stop in the middle of doing a TV interview. "That's my niece," she would say, and they had to wait until she finished talking with us.

How could this happen?

She had hidden from the Ku Klux Klan as a small girl. Her family was forced off Alabama land they rightfully owned and paid for. Then, there were those long nights when Auntie Rosa would sit up with her grandfather, a shotgun across his lap, like a sheriff and his little deputy. She had always been so fearless. But even during that time, long before she'd ever ridden a bus, much less gotten thrown off one, not a pretty hair on her head went missing. Up until the break-in, she had rarely even locked the door at Wildemere and had no problems. We'd go by to visit and knock. She'd just say, "Come in."

How could she have escaped harm for eighty-one years and be dealing with this now?

Maybe Joseph hadn't first known it was Auntie Rosa's house, but everyone else in the neighborhood knew. The streets weren't safe for him anymore. There was talk, probably even by some of us, that he should hope the police found him before another kind of "arrest" took place. Fortunately, the police got to him first. He blamed his drug problem for the episode, but it didn't help much as an excuse. We heard, later on, that he was beaten daily in prison.

THE FLIP SIDE of this terrible tragedy was an outpouring of love. Oprah Winfrey sent Auntie Rosa the most beautiful flowers. There were people driving by the house, where she was never left alone again, to give her money. One man came and handed Auntie Rosa his Purple Heart from when he'd fought in the war. Another one flew all the way to Detroit from Ireland to see about the mother of the civil rights movement. And throughout all this, Auntie Rosa never made one angry comment about the person who could've left her dead that night.

"He needs help," is what she said privately. We got the feeling that she really didn't even want him to go to jail, but that part was out of her hands. She still liked the neighborhood and, in spite of this ordeal, didn't want to leave Wildemere. But a wealthy businessman gave her a place to live at the gated Riverfront Apartments, and she was finally persuaded. The love and kindness she had always shown toward others was being rained all over her now.

A year after she died, *The Detroit News* printed an interview with Joseph, who was still serving his prison sentence ten years later. He told the reporter he cried when he found out Auntie Rosa left us on October 24, 2005.

"I will go down in history as the man who robbed Rosa Parks," he said. "I'm sorry that she died. I was hoping to get out in time to tell her I was sorry."

He didn't know Auntie Rosa had already forgiven him. He'd been a young man when he did this to her, and she loved young people. She was always teaching us how to handle anger just as much through her actions and attitudes as through her words.

It takes a lot of work to keep that meanness inside. You have to give it away.

—ROSALIND AND SHEILA

The Haircut

She had looked out for him since they were very small children. Now, they were both in their sixties, and she didn't see that as a reason for her to stop. Even when she'd come up north to start her life again, which she couldn't have done without his support, without living in his home, Auntie Rosa was still the big sister. Father was very sick now and, even though he had a devoted wife, Auntie Rosa felt like she should always share the load when it came to doing what she could for her loved ones. That's how she made a very hurtful mistake.

It really was a pretty harmless, innocent thing, certainly not the type of cruel behavior that would tear people apart from each other. That wasn't Auntie Rosa's way. She was sensitive to almost everybody's needs. This particular day was one of the rare times when she made an error in judgment. For practically his whole life, especially when he was a young man, our father had been neatly groomed and handsome. He shaved daily and, like most men from his generation, took a certain pride in his appearance. It didn't have anything to do with vanity, but back when Father was growing up, the way a man kept himself was associated with his character and how he wanted to be seen as a person. Especially during segregation, Father's peer group wanted to be viewed as every bit worthy of respect as anyone else. So when he wore his mustache, it was neatly trimmed, and his hair was cut close to his scalp.

When he reached his fifties, however, my father made one very noticeable change. He started letting his hair grow. It was the 1970s now, and a lot of younger men were wearing afros and dashikis, or sometimes headbands around long, straight bangs. Well, Father wasn't trying to imitate Jimi Hendrix, that's for sure. But something made him want to try out this new look. His hair was a similar texture to Auntie Rosa's—like heavy silk, but still full and thick—and we saw even more resemblance between them as it extended in length. Eventually, it fell all the way down to his shoulders. It was wavy and white. My mother liked it, so he wore it this way for the next few years.

After he was diagnosed with cancer, he had surgery and wasn't able to take care of himself like he had before. The medical outlook for Father made us all sad. It wouldn't be very long after the surgery before he passed. Around this time, Auntie Rosa stepped in to support my mother, who wasn't in the best of health herself. She'd had a stroke at just thirty-four, and although it had been quite a while since that time, she still struggled with respiratory illness. Even so, she was normally at the hospital with Father all day, every day after his diagnosis. I don't know how it happened that she wasn't around when Auntie Rosa came by for this particular visit, but Mother would soon regret having stepped out for the short time she did. On this occasion, Auntie Rosa brought a barber with her. Thinking it would be easier than trying to get her sick brother to a shop, and knowing he wasn't in shape enough to leave the hospital anyway, she was trying to be helpful. She had known Father purposely grew out his hair before he turned ill. Maybe she figured a fresh cut would lift his spirits. It really was a thoughtless thing to do, but my aunt didn't mean any harm.

I can't say why Father didn't speak up. He had always trusted his sister, and he might have been past caring at that point. What happened when we got back up to his room, though, was heartbreaking for my mother: She took one look at her husband and started crying. She was hurt and angry, and the stress of his sickness made her more emotional than she would have been under normal circumstances. It was really just hair, but it was something she had come to appreciate about the man she loved, and whose time with her was limited now. She felt so devastated.

When she called Auntie Rosa to let her know how upset she was, Auntie Rosa apologized right away. She said she hadn't meant to hurt my mother and that she was only doing what she could for "Brother," like she had done all of his life. My mother's reaction left an impression on Auntie Rosa, too. They had gotten along well, and there had never been competition or resentment in their relationship, the way some men's wives and sisters clash. But now my aunt had a new appreciation for the only woman who had been closer to Sylvester McCauley than she had.

"I never knew you loved him so much," Auntie Rosa said softly, before they ended their call.

It had been a misunderstanding between people who both cared deeply for one man. After Father died, they continued to bond in their own relationship and support one another whenever they could. I know Father would have liked that. When I think of how this happened—a simple act of love by one person that had unintended results for someone else—it reminds me that, for all the amazing things Auntie Rosa did, she sure wasn't perfect. She had character flaws, just like anybody else. In this case, it was my mother who showed my aunt forgiveness after my aunt had forgiven so many people at so many other times. I'm glad my mother didn't let the sorrow of losing Father become reason to hold a grudge. And I'm glad Auntie Rosa was never the type of person who felt too big to say she was sorry.

—ROSALIND

Blessing from a Bully

Back in the 1920s, in a little, dusty town down south, a skinny, quiet girl ran across a bully. The girl wasn't the type to ever go out looking for trouble. She spent most of her days helping with chores around the house; her mother was a "single parent" way before the title got to be common. If your husband left home or died, or if you found yourself in charge of a home for any reason, you didn't worry about what people called you, especially if you were poor, like the skinny, quiet girl's mother was. You just did the best you could, and your children made things a little easier, once they got big enough to work.

It was probably on one of those errands for her mother when the girl ran across Franklin. And he decided he was in the mood for a fight. Franklin was a white kid at a time when white kids had all the advantages over black ones. It would probably have been real easy for Franklin to say he caught her stealing something, or maybe that she trespassed on some property, if he just wanted to get the girl into trouble. His word would have counted more than hers. Nothing like that was good enough to satisfy him, though. On this day, he was feeling aggressive, and the girl who'd been minding her own business was in his sights without even knowing it. They traded a few words, and the girl thought Franklin's plan got to be pretty clear when she saw him ball up his fists. Unfortunately for Franklin, the skinny girl who never caused trouble wasn't the type to run away from it, either. She picked up a brick and *dared* him to lay a hand on her. Disappointed that he would have to find another punching bag, Franklin backed down. That was a story that one bully probably never got around to telling his friends.

By now, you must have figured out that Auntie Rosa was the skinny girl. She shared this story with us when we were kids and another similar one as well. Years after her run-in with Franklin, she came across another white boy—it seemed like they were the ones who always challenged her—and after some kind of confrontation, the boy pushed her. Well, she pushed him right back. That was pretty much the end. Maybe the young man just wanted to see how she would react, or he might have figured she must be crazy for having the nerve to put her hands on him! Thinking too little about what happened, Auntie Rosa made the mistake of casually mentioning it to her grandmother. That must have been the scariest thing she could have ever said, because her grandmother gave Auntie a warning she remembered for years. If she didn't learn how to treat "white folks" with more respect than that, Auntie was told, she would wind up being lynched before she turned twenty.

The way she reacted in not just one but two confrontations, let us know it never did make sense to Auntie Rosa that she shouldn't be treated the same way as anybody else—man, woman, boy, girl, white, or black. In spite of the passive image she had until her dying day, Auntie was a person who really could be pushed to the point of feeling like she had to push back. She believed in turning the other cheek, but not so she could be slapped on that one, too. At the same time, she came to understand what her grandmother was really trying to say—that when it came to fighting back, and not just against "white folks"—there was a time, a place, a right choice, and a wrong choice of weapons. Organizing and adding her brains and bravery to the brains and bravery of others is how she would battle. And she got to be a mighty soldier.

I REMEMBER when Auntie Rosa came to visit me while I was living in New Jersey. We were talking about my childhood in the late '60s. My brother and I would get beaten up every day when we were eight and nine by a boy named Michael Jones and his cousin Lo Lo.

"*Lo Lo?*" Auntie Rosa asked.

His real name was Lorenzo.

After school, they would wait for us at the corner, and we'd wonder what to do. Should we go to the other side of the street? Should we run? We always had to get by them, and they would stick out a foot, trip us to the ground, and then the punishment began. I couldn't understand why they bothered us, but I think it's because we were different. I had blond hair and green eyes, and my brother had big, shiny curls on his head; our neighbors called him "curly top." When it came to our family, it seemed like there was always some kind of negative attention from other kids, and Michael and Lo Lo were little terrorists. It was our mother who told us we wouldn't stop the bullying until we took out "the biggest one."

Michael was taller. He was the boss, and he gave Lo Lo directions. The day we attacked him, it worked out exactly the way Mother said it would. Instead of running home crying, like we usually did, we took Michael by surprise. He never expected us to defend ourselves when they walked up, ready to issue another beating. My brother and I fought for our lives, swinging and punching like wild, and he was the target. Michael was stunned, and we were scared the whole time, but he sure didn't know it! This time it was Lo Lo who ran home crying, even though we never touched him. That was the last day either one of them ever bothered a McCauley.

Auntie Rosa listened while I told that story, and she was glad I defended myself.

"Something like that happened to me," she said.

If there was one thing she believed in as much as she believed in forgiving, it was justice.

IF SHE HAD LIVED to see the day when so many children and teenagers started taking their own lives because they were bullied, it would have broken her heart. Auntie Rosa would have told them that the reasons they were teased didn't matter; it was the people doing the teasing who had the problem. Even while facing down police and a racist court—two of the worst bullies in her community—she understood that the system had a sickness. I wonder if, at times like that, during the battle of her life, Auntie Rosa thought about the boy she held off with a brick in her hand, and smiled. She could never have known it as a child, but her enemies were being used to teach her how to forgive and how to fight at the same time.

—SHEILA

On Judging Not

Even though we sometimes spent a week at a time with Auntie Rosa, Uncle Parks, and Grandma taking care of us when we were children, I never saw Auntie Rosa as a public figure until our father took us to a rally in River Rouge, Michigan, in the early '60s. I was five years old, and I mainly associated my aunt with the loving home where we often slept and where Grandma would cook down-home meals. She made cornbread in an iron skillet and cabbage with fatback, cooked long and slow. Her chicken and dumplings were my favorite. For the longest time, they were the only family we knew outside of our home with our own parents. Our world pretty much revolved around school and the neighborhood we lived in as well as the distance it took to ride back and forth to Auntie Rosa's house.

Then came that day when we went to hear her speech. I saw her being greeted and congratulated at the rally. I didn't understand all that was going on, but I was impressed.

"That's Auntie Rosa?" I asked in amazement. "Wow!" I was an introvert, and I had never been the type of child to ask a lot of questions, even if Auntie Rosa was inclined to talk about all she had done for the movement, so that experience was when I began seeing her through a different lens. That's how I learned my aunt was not only special to our family, but to her community. I started paying more attention to old newscasts at the time and thinking that the South, where she and our father had lived, was a terrible place. The picture didn't become totally clear for me right away, but I understood that, for Auntie Rosa, life had not been a walk in the park.

IN 1989, Auntie Rosa invited me to a dinner at the Jubilee National Collaborative in Hampton, Virginia, where they were recognizing her with a tribute symbol, named in her honor. A formal invitation letter that I opened read, ". . . she has chosen you to receive from her the special edition of the Rosa Parks Silver Commemorative Coin." I lived in Georgia then, and I was closer to this event than a lot of my other relatives were. I was also beginning to support some of Auntie Rosa's own programs and organizing efforts. She had resided in Virginia for a short time, so this was a bit of a homecoming for her.

By this time, I had started my own family, and I decided to take my baby daughter Bianca along for the trip, but she had an ear infection and she cried on the plane. So after trying to comfort her, I got to the dinner late. When I finally arrived, the event was under way. Auntie Rosa was at the microphone, and she acknowledged me as I walked in, carrying Bianca.

"And there's my niece Susan," she said, introducing me to the guests.

"Hi, Auntie Rosa," I replied.

"What's wrong with the baby?" she asked, noticing Bianca's

distress. The audience literally cooed. I tried not to be too much more of a distraction, and I soon found a seat.

Auntie Rosa wrote to me later, reminding me that everything happens for a reason. She was more concerned about how Bianca was feeling than what I thought of her presentation or how I felt about the program. "If you hadn't come, you wouldn't have found out that Bianca had that ear infection," her letter noted. And that was true. Bianca hadn't shown any sign of discomfort until we reached those high altitudes on the passenger jet. It was so typical of Auntie Rosa to find the hidden importance of a situation, the less obvious meaning and purpose that still held a certain value.

I would often talk to Auntie Rosa about different subjects, asking her opinions on current events. After her heart surgery, she made the decision to become a vegetarian because her doctor told her to stop eating unhealthy foods. Not only did she turn over a new dietary leaf, she also became a health food advocate and often gave me tips. Taking chlorella was one of her recommendations. I ran out to the health food store and would buy whatever she was using at the time. She had a naturopathic doctor who made up herbal concoctions, and Auntie Rosa faithfully consumed these teas and natural drinks. It was remarkable how she could adjust and adapt new habits, how she continued learning well into her senior years.

What might have been just as remarkable was her attitude toward leaders who were part of the younger generation, and her tolerance of their occasional missteps. Even when they did the most embarrassing things, I never heard Auntie Rosa condemn any of the men and women who ascended to positions of power and influence largely because of the sacrifices she and many others made decades before racial diversity in business and politics had been possible. In 1990, when the FBI got the evidence to oust Washington, D.C., mayor Marion Barry, who was one of the highest-profile black men to serve in that capacity, much of the community was ashamed. He'd been caught on tape doing drugs in an undercover sting, and the news went national. It was only January, and this was going to remain one of the biggest scandals of the year. Even Mayor Barry's friends and political colleagues were blown away.

"I'm too stunned to talk right now," Reverend Jesse Jackson told *The Washington Post*.

A city council member told the newspaper, "It's just sort of shattering. I'm just devastated."

Even the mayor's own campaign fund-raiser said, "You've got to be kidding," when he heard about Barry's arrest.

Expecting her to criticize the mayor for his moral failings, I asked Auntie Rosa what she thought of him. Her answer surprised me.

"That's a shame how they spent so much money trying to discredit this man," she said, referring to the investigation costs. "They could have used that money for programs to help people. They could be helping people, but instead they spent . . . dollars to publicly humiliate this man."

Instead of telling me how disappointed she was, or how she didn't get arrested standing up for equality just so a black mayor

Auntie Rosa and Susan in conversation in a garden
in Rancho Cucamonga, California

could get arrested on cocaine charges, she was totally nonjudg-mental. Not self-righteous, but practical. Auntie Rosa would often say, "Everybody has problems," and she would advise us, "You have to accept each person on their own merit." Some el-derly people get to a point in their lives where they become bitter, but she never did.

As fate would have it, just five years later, Mayor Barry, who had been kicked out of office after the scandal, was on the same stage as Auntie Rosa for the Million Man March in Washington, D.C. He had served time in prison, but was now apparently drug-free, and he had made an unbelievable political comeback by getting elected mayor again.

"God took me up to the mountaintop, down to the valley, and back up to the mountaintop again!" he told the vast sea of listeners gathered on the Mall at the highlight of the march.

Auntie Rosa's remarks were, as usual, brief, and she didn't draw the type of cheers and emotion that Mayor Barry did with his evangelistic flair, but I'm sure that didn't bother her in the least.

I wonder if Mayor Barry knew she had never doubted God's ability to take him "back up to the mountaintop," even when his place in the valley must have felt lowest. Auntie Rosa's refusal to judge him had been one of the many indirect, but influencing, factors that helped lift him again. Imagine what might have happened to the public's mind if the mother of the civil rights movement had made a media statement like, "This is a disgrace," after the mayor's wrongdoing came to light.

Not Auntie Rosa.

Instead, just by avoiding judgment, she and many others had been the wind beneath his wings.

—SUSAN

Day of Redemption

After a long career as a judge, governor, and even after running for president, he would be remembered by six words for the rest of his life. The phrase "segregation now, segregation tomorrow, segregation forever" would be attached to George Wallace, even in death. In 2013, the same year people all over the world celebrated what would have been Auntie Rosa's 100th birthday, the same year America mourned the fiftieth anniversary of John F. Kennedy's assassination, historians remembered that day in 1963 when Alabama's governor told the world races would always be separate in his state. Our aunt was long gone from Montgomery by then. She had been living in Michigan for years, but she heard Wallace's words, like everybody else near and far. They seemed to echo against the dividing walls of a country still crippled by its own hatred after Auntie Rosa, and so many like her, tried to give it a crutch.

Even though she was hundreds of miles away, the governor set himself up as her enemy the day he gave that speech. He set himself up as the enemy of freedom-loving people everywhere and, at the same time, he made their lives a little scarier. By coming out as a politician who said that not even the White House would change life in Alabama, he made himself a hero to racists. And when a hero to racists lines up against a hero for civil rights, it's not hard to guess what happens next.

One of them apologizes.

Well that's not what *usually* happens, but it did in 1979. A year after he left the governor's office, and several years after he was paralyzed from the waist down in an assassination attempt, Wallace met Auntie Rosa and several black leaders at St. Jude Church in Montgomery. He said he wanted to be forgiven for the things he'd said and done. It didn't end after his segregation speech—it only got worse. Six months after the speech, he stood his little, mean self in a doorway at the University of Alabama to block two black students from enrolling. He backed down after a while, but national news cameras showed just how far Wallace would go to build a reputation. Then, in 1965, he called state troopers to stop peaceful marchers from crossing a bridge from Selma to Montgomery where his headquarters were; they used tear gas and clubs, hurting marchers so badly that the incident earned the name "Bloody Sunday." This was all over voting rights, so if she lived in Alabama then, our aunt would have almost definitely been on that bridge.

At St. Jude, Wallace wanted her and everybody there to hear how sorry he was. This wasn't his only apology, either. He spent the next few years telling audiences in public and in private that he was wrong, and when he won one last term as governor, he appointed a record number of black people to jobs with the state. All this from the guy who used to let an ex-Klansman write his speeches.

As late as 1994, Wallace was still trying to let everybody know how much he had changed, like he did when he sent Auntie Rosa a signed photo of himself: "To Rosa Parks," it read. "You are a great lady."

It's hard to know if the governor, who died in 1998, was sincere in his apologies, or whether he was only doing what he thought he had to, changing with the times like any good politician. One interesting thing is that, after he retired, his foundation gave a courage award to Vivian Malone Jones, one of the students he had tried to stop from entering the university. With his health going bad and with no voters to impress, there wasn't anything much for him to gain by doing that. He made an even more personal gesture with Auntie Rosa when he tried to kiss her on the cheek that day at church, but she moved her head to dodge him.

"No, there'll be none of that," she said later.

Even forgiveness has its limits.

—ROSALIND

Strength

· ·

You can't be told what to do. You have to be
motivated—you have to feel that you
will not be pushed around.

—ROSA PARKS,
interviewed by columnist Judith Martin

It's one of the words most commonly associated with Mrs. Parks: her strength has inspired family, friends, and strangers for decades. Many have wondered how she was able to summon it on occasions when fear would be the most natural reaction for the average person. Such was her character. Such is her distinction. Not to say that Mrs. Parks' strength was of the variety that reserved itself for defining moments or historic events. It was grafted into her character, a component of the Rosa Parks prototype that has been envied but too seldom imitated. Her relatives, like much of the world, remain grateful to have felt her force.

*Painting by Asheber, based on photo
from his grandfather's visit to Detroit in 1961*

Finding Innocence (Part Two)

It took many years for me to fully understand what Auntie Rosa had said on the porch that day when she, my father, and others were discussing the murder of Emmett Till. *All white people aren't bad.*

Not that I didn't know the meaning of the words. *Good* and *bad* had clear definitions for me and my brothers and sisters, like for most children during that time. But how could *white people* not be "bad"? They were the ones who took Auntie Rosa to jail. They were the ones who killed a little boy. For *whistling*! I had heard Auntie Rosa and been soothed by her attention, but it wasn't like I just dried my tears and forgot all about the episode. Emmett Till's dead body and the adults' reactions gave me more information about the world than my mind could fully process. It really shook me.

What's even scarier is recognizing now, more than fifty years later, what the reason for that gathering on the porch actually was. I heard the whole conversation, but I didn't have a frame of reference for terms like *protest* and *organize*. I just remember the emotion in their voices. The adults had all been called there to talk Auntie Rosa out of going down South for a demonstration. She and Uncle Parks had just settled into their own house with our grandmother, and her days of protesting were over, so everybody thought. But that year, a writer from Alabama published a story in *Look*, telling how one of Emmett Till's killers said he didn't regret the murder. After the trial, he had confessed and even been paid money to do the interview! People were organizing in response to the hatred and violence that left both of Emmett's killers free to brag about what they'd done once the jury found them not guilty. It was a shock to the family that Auntie Rosa actually wanted to put herself in danger by getting in the middle of all this. Even if the cause had been a less controversial one, she was still Rosa Parks, the woman whose face was on the front page of newspapers and on TV screens around the world not even two years earlier.

It turned out that the whole reason our father drove over there was to try to help the others talk Auntie Rosa out of getting involved. Grandma was in tears. Everybody, including Uncle Parks, was against the idea of her going. They pleaded. No one thought she would come back alive if she left Detroit. Emmett's gruesome photo was a reminder of what could happen if you became a target of racism, but Auntie Rosa was so headstrong. What finally led everybody off the porch and into the house was that they gave up. In the end, Auntie Rosa didn't go to the rally, for whatever reason, but it wasn't because they had changed her mind; it was because *she* changed her mind. That was Auntie Rosa.

As an adult now, I find it amazing that she was able to correct my statement about hating white people. She was strong enough to stand up to every adult in the family confronting her, but caring enough to console me just minutes later. To this day, I know people my age who are intolerant of other races but who haven't seen half of what Auntie Rosa saw in her lifetime. And she was prepared to go risk her life a second time to fight, not against a color, but against a wrongdoing. She separated the evil from the evildoers. In this way, I believe her ability to forgive was directly connected to her strength.

That Auntie Rosa could see the difference between the consequences of hurt and the shortcomings of those who caused it made her one of the strongest people I have ever known.

—DEBORAH

My First Life Coach

For as long as I can remember, I felt very proud to be part of the McCauley family. Between Auntie Rosa and my father, Asheber, we were always well entertained. My family and I frequently visited her cozy house. This is when our relationship felt the most personal and meaningful to me. I would eat fresh cherries from the table and brush her long, silver hair as we talked. I looked forward to these visits. They were a pleasant sanctuary for me, like our own little intimate retreat. Out in the world, on the other hand, Auntie Rosa was always very clear in telling me I would have to prepare myself.

"Being a woman is not easy," she cautioned. She wanted me to remember that life is not a game. At a young age, I received these thoughts to digest in ways that would leave me thinking. It might have seemed like sophisticated conversation for a child in elementary school, but she actually never talked over my head. Another time, when my brother attended a traditional African rite-of-passage ceremony, Auntie Rosa took that opportunity to share women's elder wisdom with me. She told me to always claim my voice by speaking my mind, to be strong, and to keep my goals in sight. These talks were like Auntie Rosa's version of life coaching—nothing that was meant to punish or chastise, but simply instructions to help mentally condition me for the future she knew lay ahead.

Her path was one most people could not have traveled. She

was a veteran of hard times and a true authority on how to get through them. I was the baby she'd met and watched grow from the crib. Her example made big contributions to my life. She was my grand-aunt, but I also found in her a mentor because of her motivating yet gentle spirit. Auntie Rosa had been born poor and grown rich with influence. She had been treated like a peasant and then walked with a king. It wouldn't be too long before I grew up and learned that she was right when she said being a woman wasn't easy. Remembering her presence and her words has given me one of the greatest advantages.

—ZAKIYA

Higher Ground

Tears streamed down her face, but they didn't come from sadness.

In fact, this was probably one of the moments when Auntie Rosa was most content. She was perfectly quiet. Not sobbing or sniffling. We were sitting together in church—one of the few places where, perhaps, Auntie Rosa felt she could completely release the load of her pressures, concerns, and any anxiety that many years of being a brick wall for countless others must have built up inside her soul. Her tears were her release, but not the form of release that came from feeling emotionally overwhelmed. No, when Auntie Rosa cried those silent brooks, they were clearly streams of comfort. The comfort of knowing that a power greater than her had not once left her alone and would continue to carry and protect her until the end of her days.

After all, she was only human. But Auntie Rosa was a human who had sometimes carried on her slender frame the weight of the whole world. Her tears weren't those of a fragile woman, but those of a woman who had been bruised and cut by life's jagged rocks and still refused to let herself be broken. Auntie Rosa's tears were her spiritual meditation.

PROBABLY VERY FEW PEOPLE would find it surprising to know she was a Christian woman. She had once introduced a Georgia preacher, named Martin Luther King, as "our leader" not long before he took the microphone for an Alabama speech. Her upbringing and beliefs closely aligned with Dr. King's teaching of spiritual principles in the resistance front, of which she became a critical part, though she had also known the influence of Marcus Garvey. Not many ever saw the quiet, private worship that she practiced, or had the privilege we had of joining her in these times she held sacred. She wasn't religious in the way "Bible-thumpers" tend to be, but she was traditional in her view of God as the greatest source of power. She followed the path of Christ and picked up her cross daily. African Methodist Episcopal—the denomination started by former slaves determined to claim a Creator that loved them equally to whites, who wouldn't even set aside discrimination in church—appealed to Auntie Rosa. The ancestors of her creed knew resistance had a liberating, spiritual value.

Auntie Rosa attended St. Matthew A.M.E. on a regular basis. She had her faith, and we often saw her pray silently during the worship service. It was the way of the McCauley women to be composed—very strong, but also very prim and proper. A lot of us loved going to church with her. Sometimes the younger girls in the family would dress up in little lace socks and white gloves. Auntie Rosa didn't allow the children to sit in the back and chew gum. Attending service with her meant you observed decorum. She believed in putting God first and loving others, but not forgetting to love yourself. She said the Creator gave us the power to learn, the ability to tolerate people's faults, and the opportunity to fully use our gifts and skills to better ourselves. She also said that anyone can move a mountain if they do what is right. All of it was Auntie Rosa's philosophy based on her faith and Christian principles. It was what she truly believed and how she lived each day, with the grace, respect, and honesty she promoted.

Auntie Rosa was a good example of the Bible scriptures where Jesus says you have to be in the world, but not of the world. She really didn't carry on or get familiar with many people, but God had to pick somebody to do his work. And when our aunt felt she had been chosen, she didn't hesitate. We're sure her faith in a higher power is what carried her. It was unwavering. In her darkest hours, she was never alone because God stayed by her side.

Largely due to its connection to the civil rights movement, the church continued to embrace Auntie Rosa throughout her life, frequently inviting her to their community engagements, anniversary events, and other special programs. Congregations all over the country welcomed her for years, often asking her to speak or accept tributes. Once, Auntie Rosa took the opportunity to appear at a church with her mother and show appreciation for the leading lady in her life on Mother's Day. The congregation members were all moved to see their role model celebrating the woman who helped shape Rosa Parks into who she became.

In our aunt's view, church leaders and clergy were also people of action, like Dr. King, Ralph Abernathy, and a young Jesse Jackson had all been when she was on the battlefront. That's why she was glad to meet Pope John Paul II in St. Louis in 1999. She was eighty-five then and not getting around as well, but she made the trip to Cathedral Basilica and gave him a copy of her book. He was calling for racial harmony in a prayer service to help usher in the year, and she believed all religions should have a role in promoting goodwill. The church was not only a source of Auntie Rosa's spiritual strength, but also a place where she found like-minded people who shared her commitment to justice throughout the world.

One letter she received gives an idea of how she was viewed by fellow believers. The note, dated March 6, 1957, is written from Philadelphia by a man identified as George A. Singleton, and it reads, in part: "Dear Mrs. Parks . . . By the grace of God, you have written your name high in the halls of fame by your courage and perseverance for first-class citizenship." She received this kind of praise from clergy and congregation members far and wide, Jewish and gentile people of faith. Sadly, though, she some-times got reports of how spiritual freedom fighters suffered unbe-lievable loss for standing on their beliefs, like in the case of Reverend Joseph DeLaine. A minister in Auntie Rosa's A.M.E. denomination, he helped fight for children to get bus transporta-tion because some of them walked as far as eight miles each way to school. The segregated Clarendon County, South Carolina, district said black families didn't pay as many taxes as white fam-ilies did, and that the white tax base shouldn't be used to support transportation for students of color. Reverend DeLaine fought continuously and eventually had the school bus issue included with the 1954 Supreme Court school desegregation case, but Auntie Rosa's letter from George Singleton explained the price he paid: "His house, church and Bible were burned to the ground. He lost more than anyone in the fight, and today he is homeless."

Auntie Rosa would long outlive spiritual leaders like King and Malcolm X, who she also met and respected. And she would share the shock of many communities that suffered chilling, racially motivated arsons during the 1990s as they watched their parishes burn down, just like Reverend DeLaine's parish had burned. But she remained a churchgoer for as long as her health would let her, refusing to let anything put distance between her faith and her religious foundation. When she began staying on the West Coast for several months a year, she still found her way to Sunday ser-vices. As a driving force in her life, Auntie Rosa's spirituality is what made her even more powerful than her own stubborn will. She believed, and kept on believing. She had walked through the valley of the shadow of death more than once and feared no evil. Faith was the covering that helped Auntie Rosa make an impact on people everywhere she went.

—RHEA, EDRIA, LONNIE, ROBERT, AND ZAKIYA

Branding of an Icon

With all the adulation and praise Auntie Rosa received for so much of her long life, we had to sometimes wonder if she ever got used to it. Her reactions were almost always the same, no matter who she encountered. She was just as gracious toward strangers who approached her as she was toward friends she'd known for years, and she was just as gracious toward friends as she was toward all of the many mayors and world leaders she had the privilege of meeting. Much too often to count, she received invitations to major award ceremonies, speeches, dinners, tribute galas, and corporate events where her name was on the same guest list as people like Jesse Jackson, Maya Angelou, and Stevie Wonder, who sang his famous version of "Happy Birthday" to Auntie Rosa when she turned eighty-nine. The serenade took place at the premiere of a made-for-TV movie based on her life. Throughout all these types of experiences, Auntie Rosa was the same person in the company of celebrities and dignitaries that she was when she spoke to small church congregations and in elementary school classrooms. In fact, she might have actually given a little more of herself in the classroom setting than she gave to the "who's who" crowd because she adored children and saw so much hope in them. She carried herself in a consistent manner, no matter who was around. Auntie Rosa even introduced us to well-known entertainment personalities like Harry Belafonte, Ossie Davis, and Dick Gregory. She wouldn't have known how to go about putting on airs or making distinctions in the way she treated people like them compared with how she treated the mailman. She was as unassuming as anyone you've ever met.

One story that stands out is the time when she had the opportunity to meet South African leader Nelson Mandela in 1990 after he'd gotten out of prison. Mandela had been jailed for twenty-seven years for doing something similar in South Africa to what Auntie Rosa had done in Alabama and fighting the racist system of apartheid segregation. Seven years after Auntie Rosa was arrested, Mandela was taken into custody across the ocean for his aggressive activism against a government that sanctioned racism against South African blacks. In a way, he and Auntie were like kindred spirits, but Mandela's journey toward freedom was blocked when he was tried and convicted, then given a life sentence of incarceration for trying to overthrow the system that oppressed him. While he couldn't continue helping to mobilize the movement the way Auntie Rosa did after 1955, his sacrifice gained attention around the world. He became an international hero, and his freedom was on the minds of so many people near and far, people like Auntie Rosa who had never been anywhere near South Africa. When his release was announced, it was a day of celebration in cities and countries across every continent. Mandela visited Detroit and spoke at the old Tiger Stadium baseball park, where Auntie Rosa helped rally the crowd. She even carried a bullhorn. She was so eager and excited to shake his hand and congratulate him. But with the eyes of the entire community on Mandela that day, we heard that some of his first words to our aunt were, "I wanted to meet *you*." Auntie Rosa's contributions to freedom would later be recognized at the Nelson Mandela Museum in Ngaphezulu, South Africa.

In instances like this, Aunt Rosa epitomized the civil rights icon status that she became identified with during her later years. It wasn't a title she sought for herself, and none of it was treatment she demanded from the public. Rather, it was the natural result of how she continued to demonstrate her commitment to the values she became known for when she first painted her name onto the broad canvas of history. Even as an elderly woman, she remained quite vocal on issues of social justice, racial inequality, and unfair labor practices. These were the things that fueled her. Never once did she personally request that a bust be carved in her image or a parade be held in her honor. We watched her receive medals and attend dedications in her name. You can't drive through Detroit or Montgomery, where there are so many tributes and monuments of various kinds, and not be reminded that Auntie Rosa once called these places home, that she had both blended in with the populations there and done extraordinary things for those same populations through her selflessness. Auntie Rosa never considered herself part of a community without adding something to it. Her rewards and joy came from seeing justice done and from knowing others were putting forth action, just as she did, whenever and wherever action was warranted. She never required the formal thanks or impressive flattery that was so often thrown her way. All Auntie Rosa wanted was the same basic courtesy and respect that she gave.

That isn't to say Auntie didn't appreciate any of the attention she received. She was accommodating and appreciative when an organization wanted to give her a special honor. She usually accepted all of the invitations she could because she saw every public appearance as a way to remind those present that the struggle should continue until no one possessed a single right that a person of a different race, age, sex, or background didn't possess, too. This was the *real* Auntie Rosa. It wasn't a persona she put on or took off like a work uniform. Her thoughts were always geared toward what she, personally, could do to promote more favorable conditions for all of us to live in, and if she couldn't encourage someone else to do the same, it would never be from a lack of effort.

Sometimes we enjoyed getting a glimpse of how other people viewed the woman we'd known for our whole lives, like when *The Rosa Parks Story*, starring Angela Bassett, aired on television. There's a scene when the actress playing Auntie as a teenager runs outside in her nightgown, with her hair down, laughing and acting silly. Well, what *we* thought was silly was the idea of Auntie Rosa ever doing anything like that. We laughed so hard because Grandma would have never let her daughter carry on that way, and Auntie Rosa knew better. Grandma even fussed at us about wearing pants or shorts instead of dresses, showing our skin, and things like that, and this was long after Auntie Rosa's years as a young lady. Auntie Rosa reiterated what Grandma instilled in her when she told her nieces we should always act like ladies, no matter the situation.

Details like the young actress's wardrobe were pretty harmless, overall, since the representation of Auntie Rosa's character is what mattered more than anything. Conducting herself like a true servant whose main priority every morning she woke up was to see how she could help someone took commitment, yet she didn't seem to feel as if she was holding herself to a high standard. Nor did she judge people who hadn't reached the level of awareness she had reached, even though she thought we all shared responsibility for stepping up. If you criticized someone in her presence, she would say, "You should just pray for them. Maybe they're doing the best they can." For a woman who had overcome so much on her own, she was extremely understanding toward people who had not yet overcome. Her ability to see everyone for the good that he or she had potential to offer made her patient, even when they weren't quite ready to act. This was a fascinating quality of someone who didn't have a hesitant bone in her own body. Maybe she knew that a person's best is offered only when the person is comfortable and confident in a decision.

Just as Auntie Rosa could be passionate, she had an amazing ability to be objective. If she felt something wasn't practical, she would say so, and a lot of times, hers was the clearest voice of reason. Although she never shared these types of details with us, it's not hard to imagine the role she played in her days of organizing with the NAACP. Immediately after the bus incident, her demeanor was probably no different from what it had been the entire day, though she'd just made a move that would change American history. We can imagine Auntie Rosa calmly talking with E. D. Nixon and the other organizers about the next steps that would be taken to carry their momentum forward. Surely she would have been concise with her words, as she typically was, debriefing everyone on details of exactly what had happened. When asked for her input, she would have given it freely and been prepared to help contribute to the planning of the bus boycott. She would have been ready to serve the community, just as she had for all those years when she was NAACP secretary. It was a given that Auntie Rosa could be counted on, not only to support the boycott for that long year of staying off buses that followed her arrest, but to encourage everybody else she knew to walk, hitch rides, or carpool in playing their part to support the mass protest. The Auntie Rosa we knew would have stayed as active behind the scenes as she possibly could have, even though her brave moment out front would have fully entitled her to watch the battle's outcome from that point on, in many people's minds. That wasn't even an option for Auntie Rosa—she was indicted a couple months after refusing to give up her seat and arrested again, with eighty-eight other people accused of violating a state law against *boycotts*. It was a charge designed by Montgomery authorities to discourage people from continuing to disrupt the status quo, and the protest was just eleven weeks old. There would be other attempts to turn Auntie Rosa and the others around, like when there was an increase in the cab fares some residents used in place of bus rides, but they persevered.

For a lot of people, the consistent pressure and harassment would have been too much to handle. They were living through dangerous times. A wrong glance could have huge consequences. Auntie Rosa seemed more motivated by the consequences of what might become of society if she didn't put forth efforts to change it. Her anxious moments came more from imagining how much worse off things would be if she failed to protest than from fearing how much worse off she might be, individually, after protesting. When all has been said and done about measuring motives for what Auntie Rosa did in 1955 and during the forty years that followed, it's clear to her family that she pressed forward to keep the bad times from standing still. We stress to our children more than the fact that she participated in the struggle; through her, they can learn how to apply the principles from that era to their own experiences. Hopefully, they never have to get arrested or have their reputations attacked like Auntie Rosa and so many others on the frontline with her did, but they can, at least, know the virtues of conviction. Taking strong positions, whether privately or on public stages, gave her a greater sense of security than running away ever could.

—ROSALIND, SUSAN, AND LONNIE

To Be Continued

She was just getting home from Japan.

Japan.

Auntie Rosa was truly loved worldwide. She had flown all the way there to receive an honorary degree sometime around 1994. I admired her so much, and I was proud that people all the way on the other side of the globe were still recognizing her importance after so many decades. My children and my siblings' children all grew up knowing the importance of the civil rights movement and the role Auntie Rosa played in it. What was so great for our younger generation of McCauleys was that she was still alive and well enough for them to touch and connect with her. They didn't have to imagine Auntie Rosa based on old, fuzzy newsreel images or photos in their classroom textbooks.

But I had a concern. She was making frequent trips, sometimes long ones like this visit to Japan had been, and I wondered if she should keep going at this pace. She was in her early eighties now, a time when even the healthiest people who live that long start taking it easy. I knew she still had a passion for working and she wasn't ready to become a shut-in or one of those senior citizens who didn't go anywhere except church, and I could respect that, but I felt like I should tell her my thoughts. It had been on my mind for a while, so that's what I did.

When Auntie Rosa called to tell me she had made it home, I let her know I would be stopping by to see her in a few days. Once I was able to sit with her in person, I was surprised to hear her say she was getting ready to leave town again.

"Auntie Rosa," I said, "don't you think it's time to start slowing down a little?"

We didn't really second-guess her decisions, but I had only asked the question out of love. It was important that I try to show the same interest in her well-being that she had always shown in mine, in all of ours. Auntie Rosa looked at me, and I could tell my thought had probably never crossed her mind.

"I'm going to do this until I can't do it anymore," she said. "There's still a lot to do, especially for the youth, and I will as long as I can."

The tone of her response felt so firm, I knew it was the end of the conversation. And things went just the way she said they would. Unfortunately, it wasn't too much longer before her failing health did force Auntie Rosa to slow down, but in the few years that she managed to keep traveling, her appearances included some major ones. In 1996, she went to Washington to receive the Presidential Medal of Freedom, and three years later, the Congressional Gold Medal.

"This medal is encouragement for all of us to continue until all have rights," she told the audience of about 650 people.

There, at age eighty-six, she was taking another opportunity to let people know what she had told me at her house that day— that she would continue speaking out and using her name for whatever good it might bring about. More and more, she needed help getting around, and she never talked for long periods, but just being in the same room with her gave a lot of people inspiration. Watching her smile or shaking her hand was a big thrill, even to presidents, senators, and community leaders who had power and influence, but who had, themselves, grown up reading about how Auntie Rosa took her proud stand. Maybe she knew that showing her face to the public could serve as a reminder of what one person can do to change circumstances that affect us all.

Now, I'm glad Auntie Rosa decided to follow her mind. I would have regretted it myself if she stopped doing what was most important to her just to put her family's worries to rest. After all, she had made clothes for us, fed us, and given us her support in whatever ways she was able to. She had been more involved in our lives than a lot of nieces and nephews ever experience from an aunt. Behind spreading her energies between so many people for so long, she deserved to spend her remaining active years doing whatever she pleased. It was everybody's good fortune that what she chose was to move ahead on her journey.

—ROSALIND

Our Champion

During the times when Auntie Rosa was coming up, boxers became increasingly popular in the black community. There was Jersey Joe Walcott and Sugar Ray Robinson. Joe Louis and Floyd Patterson. Long after Auntie Rosa's name was well known, there was even Muhammad Ali, who owed a lot of his popularity to the hope and dignity that grew out of the civil rights movement. Although they were sportsmen and not politicians, the high profile of fighters like these was inspiring to people of color who were told they were less talented and less intelligent than others living in segregated America. Joe Louis became a hero even for many white folks when he fought Max Schmeling in the 1930s. This was around the time of Hitler's rise and the growing tension between America and Germany, the nation Schmeling represented. It was considered more than just a heavyweight fight when those two stepped into the ring; it represented a face-off between world powers. And it was a new emotion for white Americans to hope a black man could beat a white one at *anything*. In his autobiography, *The Collected Works of Langston Hughes: I Wonder as I Wander*, Hughes described how much of a hero to blacks the "Brown Bomber" was: "I do not believe Negro America has ever before, or since, had a national hero like Joe Louis. As he went up the ladder toward the championship, and after he became champion, winning fight after fight, Louis became a kind of symbol of all that Negroes had always dreamed of in American life."

When the Bomber had a match, you could almost always tell by how silent it became in black neighborhoods where, in house after house, from corner to corner, families were huddled around their radios to cheer him on. If he lost, it was felt by thousands, like it was when Schmeling knocked him out. "After the fight, which I attended," Hughes wrote, "I walked down Second Avenue and saw grown men weeping like children, and women sitting on the curbs with their heads in their hands." Louis won their second match, redeeming himself and earning praise from both black and white fans. By 1974, Auntie Rosa and Joe Louis would have a grand-nephew in common when Sylvester Jr.'s son Lonnie was born; Lonnie's mother, Joan, who also had a daughter, Urana, is the boxing legend's niece.

But the champ and Auntie Rosa share more than a younger generation of relatives. As a focal point for people who wanted justice, she, like him, was a symbol. The black community's sense of power was lifted when she won her public fight, triggering the support of marginalized people around the country. And eventually, like they embraced Joe Louis, a tremendous number of whites celebrated Auntie Rosa. Some even called her the person they most admired.

Auntie Rosa was a champion in a dress.

What a lot of people often overlook, however, is that her life wasn't only dedicated to racial equality. She was a champion for a number of causes: education, community empowerment, and women's rights, just to name a few. One example was the case of Recy Taylor, who was raped by six men as she walked home from an evening church service in Abbeville, Alabama, a decade before the civil rights movement. Auntie Rosa sought her out and interviewed her on behalf of the NAACP, guiding her through the process of how to hold these men responsible. When a jury wouldn't indict them, even after reported confessions, Auntie helped launch a committee to spread the word. Soon, Governor Chauncey Sparks started getting petitions and thousands of postcards demanding justice. He tried to do something, too, but he couldn't force any action against the rapists without juror support. Auntie Rosa's efforts weren't just legal; she helped Recy and her family find temporary boarding outside Abbeville after they were threatened. All this happened in 1944, close to a dozen years before the bus boycott, and Auntie Rosa had already sent ripples way up into the governor's office.

She has been an icon for women mainly because she demonstrated their capabilities. Women see Auntie Rosa in exactly the way she wanted to be seen as one person who did only what she knew was right. That summed up her basic philosophy, and her belief was that everyone has it within them to do the same. But a lot of women also view her as proof that they don't have to wait on a man to take the lead. She wasn't necessarily trying to send these types of messages, as much as she was always following her own conscience. It has been documented that Auntie Rosa was the first female member of the Montgomery NAACP, but her goal wasn't trailblazing; it was world-changing.

People associate power with wealth, rank, and status, but none of that is it. Strength comes from the inside, and Auntie Rosa was filled with it. It didn't only show in the big moments most people have read about or seen portrayed in movies and on PBS programs; it showed in the way she conducted herself for most of her ninety-two long years. Not even the racists who never got over their hatred for Auntie Rosa, after what they saw as an unforgivable act of defiance, could call her weak. She was a fine woman, one whose pride never got in the way of her progress. When she needed help, she would accept it, although she wasn't necessarily quick to ask. Auntie Rosa wasn't easily shamed when it came to letting it be known that she sometimes had hard times.

Just like they loved sporting champions, a lot of people loved her, but few of them ever knew much of her life as a girl or young woman. Someone wrote that Auntie Rosa once picked cotton to earn spending money, but that wasn't true. She picked cotton just to survive. She had known difficult times and lived through many years of them, which is probably why she couldn't be easily intimidated. It was clear to us that she had developed a healthy self-esteem in order to do the incredible things no one would have ever expected from a poor child who wasn't born with a single personal advantage. If not for her strong constitution, she could have easily settled for what little bit society said she was entitled to. Instead, when she was knocked down, like Joe Louis, she got up and demanded a rematch; whether the fight was about voting, integration, or any other cause, she came back swinging hard.

Until she won.

—RHEA, SHIRLEY, AND ROBERT

Encouragement

*It has been a long, hard struggle; we have won
much and have much more to win. . . .*

—ROSA PARKS,
1957 letter seeking support for the NAACP

Victory had a bittersweet taste for the diminutive, dignified seamstress who faced down the beast of racism by refusing to give up her bus seat. After the Montgomery boycott put public segregation into a permanent chokehold, Rosa Parks' courage afforded her heroine status throughout the world. But life at home for the woman who'd once sharecropped to survive would never be the same. Gone were E. D. Nixon and the organizers who'd sprung into activism and helped free her from police custody the day of her arrest; gone were the throngs of media, leaving her and husband, Raymond, to try returning to normalcy in KKK country among violently vindictive bigots. Where do soldiers find their sanctuary? In Mrs. Parks' case, it was Detroit, where her younger brother, Sylvester McCauley, and his wife, Daisy, had relocated to raise their children. Not only did the move potentially save Mrs. Parks' life from any number of Southerners who regarded her as a marked woman, it also placed her among

loved ones, by whom she'd eventually be viewed as a matri-
arch and personal role model.

In this capacity, she accomplished through spoken words
and silent examples more than most of the adults her nieces
and nephews encountered throughout their lives. In addition to
their parents, the McCauley children viewed Mrs. Parks as
their teacher and counselor. She could be as firm as a drill
sergeant but without ever raising her voice. She could also be
subtle in her influence while still making her impact apparent.
Like a calm wind. For the late Sylvester McCauley Jr., a full
lifetime has passed since the day his aunt showed up in De-
troit to become a guide and surrogate parent, long after Syl-
vester Sr. and Daisy left to join the ancestors. The remaining
siblings continue to benefit from the encouragement their aunt
gave so generously before she was reunited with "Brother,"
Daisy, and Sylvester Jr. for a second time.

More Than a Pen Pal

If I didn't write her or she didn't write me, we would call each
other.

The time just before I moved to Berlin with my husband, who
was in the military, was pretty traumatic for me. My mother had
died, and I was already grieving that loss, let alone feeling some
separation anxiety about going all the way to Germany, where I
would be farther away from the rest of my family than I ever had

been. Then, in what felt like the blink of an eye, I was a mother for the first time and, since mine was gone, I was so grateful Auntie Rosa was there to advise me. I didn't even have a second thought about who I would turn to for guidance and counseling about all the major changes and challenges appearing so suddenly in my life.

"Call me. Write me," she had said. "I'll help you get through it."

That's when a lot of our letter exchanges really began. It was usually general stuff. "How are you feeling?" "This is how I'm feeling . . ." But I also found myself looking in Auntie Rosa's direction when I felt so overwhelmed that I sometimes didn't know my next step. As we relocated, I had problems with my marriage, and money issues weren't far behind. At some point, writing letters became the solution not only because I felt the need to stay connected to her, but because our phone got turned off.

I was always honest with her when things were fine and when things were a struggle. I can even admit that I was a crybaby when times were most tough. It seemed that no matter what the crisis, Auntie Rosa found ways to give me wisdom and comfort. "I'll help you get through it." She always did. The one thing she wasn't ever about to do was let me stay discouraged. And I'm grateful, too, that she reminded me not to lose sight of myself as I took on new responsibilities. I am a visual artist, and she didn't ever want me to become so consumed with other obligations that I started to neglect my gift.

"Remember who *you* are," she would say in a way that sounded both simple and profound.

I truly owe a debt to Auntie Rosa. Through many letters and

Dec. 13, 1996

Dear Shirley,

I should have answered your letter before now. I just received these pictures and I misplaced your letter.

I hope you and the girls will have a Merry Christmas and Happy New Year.

I am leaving tomorrow to go south, for a while.

Love from
Aunt Rosa

Rosa L. Parks
9311 Wildemere
Detroit, Michigan 48206
(313) 898-6776

July 17, 1998

Dear Shirley,

I am sorry that I did not see you when you were here. We went out of Detroit, and did not get back in time to see you. Elaine wants to give this little badge to you.

I hope to see you when you come back this way again.

Love from,
Your Aunt Rosa

many conversations over the years, she was a lifeline of peace and stability during some of the tremors that shook my faith in myself. She was a true nurturer, an emotional support bank. I'm so glad to have been a member. I can only imagine how many times I might have crumbled under the weight of stress if I wasn't able to open a letter from her, or sit down and write one that I knew she'd quickly respond to. Even with countless miles between us, I could always feel the blessings of her warmth.

—SHIRLEY

Left to right: Nikki and Faye (Shirley's daughters),
Auntie Rosa, Shirley McCauley.
Taken at Fairlane Mall in Dearborn, Michigan, in 1994.
Photo by Monica Morgan.

Fallen Warrior

He was the type of person you'd hardly ever hear a negative word spoken about. Even if you never had the chance to know him well, you wished you had after only briefly being around him. Adisa was dead now, at only twenty-five, and Auntie Rosa was heartbroken. She told the Associated Press, "He was just as close to me as if he were my own grandson. I felt that way about him, and that's how he felt about me."

He had been a normal Detroit teenager with normal Detroit teenager friends. He went to public school, mostly avoiding peer pressure and staying out of trouble. Somewhere along the short path of his life, he had an awakening. He took the first name Adisa—"one who makes his meaning clear"—and the last name Foluke—"under God's protection." He started wearing African clothes and participated in mentoring programs for teenagers, like those designed to help deter them from prison. Through family members who had started assisting her, he met and became fond of Auntie Rosa. Soon he was a member of the Rosa and Raymond Parks Institute for Self Development staff.

That's how he wound up on the bus that terrible day.

SOME OF THE FAMILY first met him at Auntie Rosa's new place in the Riverfront Apartments in the mid-1990s. It was around the Fourth of July, and two of Auntie's grandnephews wanted to see the fireworks downtown. Well, they were too small to be in the crowd of thousands that always filled up Hart Plaza to get the best view in the city on a pleasant night, in the open air with a clear view of the starry sky. Sometimes fighting and craziness broke out down there, and it wasn't the type of scene any parent would want to have to break away from with little children to drag along, if this was one of those occasions. Plus, it was a weeknight, which meant that traffic heading out of downtown could add an hour to the time it took getting to bed before work and school the next day. But Terrence and Tommy wanted to watch the action, so Auntie Rosa got a call in the afternoon, asking her if it was okay to bring them out to her high-rise with its perfect view of the waterfront skyline. Of course, she said yes.

What we didn't know was that the elevators in her building were out of order that day and there was a lot of exercise waiting on us, since Auntie Rosa lived on the thirteenth floor. Terrence and Tommy hugged her and said hi when they walked into her place where Adisa was visiting, along with his aunt, who was Auntie Rosa's personal aide. She and Auntie Rosa were in the kitchen cooking spinach, or maybe squash. It was something that needed butter, and they didn't have any butter—which meant the first trip down those thirteen flights from Auntie Rosa's unit to the building convenience store.

Adisa came along for the mission. He was such a nice fellow, and he seemed happy to do whatever he could to help our aunt. There was mostly just small talk between us, but it was easy to see that he was a pleasant young man. We bought the butter and hiked back up the mountain of stairs to provide the missing ingredient for dinner. After everybody was settled and it got closer to the time when the first flare would blast off, we made the journey back downstairs again and walked over to the Plaza, leaving Terrence and Tommy behind to watch from Auntie Rosa's huge front window. Adisa was a gentleman and a friendly escort. It was a really nice show. The fireworks looked like bright ribbons spread across the night.

That evening with Adisa, this new face in our aunt's inner circle, would be the only one we'd have to remember of him.

EVEN BEFORE THE CRASH, there had been talk of how tired the driver was. A friend who worked for the local news station was doing some freelance work and taping a documentary on "Pathways to Freedom," the historical tour that our aunt's institute sponsored every year to teach young people about the Underground Railroad. They'd fill up a bus and ride throughout the South to retrace the route enslaved men and women traveled to freedom. The documentary was being recorded so it could be used as a fund-raiser, and the main bus driver was one of the people interviewed. The full route of the tour was fifteen states and 40,000 miles, and the driver said he was exhausted. It came out in the news later that he had only gotten four hours of rest that entire day in July 1997 before the bus went off the road into a chilly Virginia river. We found out there were no skid marks or signs he ever tried to stop, which immediately told us he had dozed off at the wheel. The driver and thirty-four people, including chaperones, had injuries.

Poor Adisa was the only one to lose his life.

Auntie Rosa grieved. If she had been given a million years to ponder the trip, she probably still would never have imagined anything like this happening. She had started letting her staff—people like Adisa himself—take care of details when it came to the institute's programming, so hiring and relieving bus drivers would never have been anything she directly handled. It seemed that she started to change after the accident. If she spoke, her voice would sometimes trail off. Her attention seemed to get shorter. She had been interviewed, and told reporters that she hoped the children who "survived" the accident would be comfortable continuing with the tour. But in private, her mood was sometimes hard to read.

For their part, the kids really seemed like they'd already learned from Auntie Rosa's determination. One of them was quoted in the media as saying the tour leaders taught them that those riding the bus weren't "free" until they reached the end of the route in Canada, where it had ended for escaped slaves. As far as she was concerned, the ancestors had made it to freedom and so would she. A twelve-year-old boy said he wanted to reboard a new bus in Detroit in Adisa's memory. "He told us to rise to the occasion, no matter what the circumstance," read the child's *Richmond Times-Dispatch* quote.

They were amazing young people. Lloyd Colar, who had a broken finger, told the *Chicago Tribune*: "I'll go on because the slaves went on. If they had given up every time they faced adversity where would we be now?" If listening to Adisa taught them this way of thinking, Adisa must have paid a lot of attention to Auntie Rosa.

DAYS AND WEEKS PASSED after the accident, and Auntie Rosa probably realized, like she always used to say, that there was still work to be done. With Adisa's memory in her heart, she went back to devoting time to the institute. We barely got to know him at all, and she had already come to view him as a family member. He was there watching the front door on the day after she was robbed, refusing to let our youngest sister, Cheryl, into Auntie Rosa's house because he hadn't met her and wasn't taking any chances. He and Cheryl had a few heated words and, somehow, things took care of themselves without it getting too ugly between the blood niece and the adopted relative. Now, there would be kind of a role reversal for Adisa and Auntie Rosa. Even though he'd worked for her, she would have to be the one to carry on her "grandson's" efforts. It was part of her journey as an elder warrior.

And warriors sometimes lose companions.

—SHEILA AND SUSAN

Multiple Connections

It might seem like a funny thing to admit, but I didn't discover who Auntie Rosa *really* was until third grade. Just as she was with all her other nephews and nieces, she was close to my mom. When my mother was a teenager, she regularly took the bus to visit Auntie Rosa at work when she was an aide in Congressman Conyers' downtown office. My mother would get out of class on a given day, pack up her books, throw on her coat, and head straight to where she knew she could find one of her favorite relatives. A lot of times, she'd just do homework while Auntie Rosa was busy handling whatever duties the congressman might have assigned her. Mom was so fond of her aunt's company that it didn't take a lot to keep her entertained, and Auntie Rosa didn't mind having her niece tag along. Other times, they might have lunch or sip tea together like two old friends. It was a relationship my mother cherished throughout her life.

That day in elementary school was the first time I was able to draw a connection. We were studying the civil rights movement, and my textbook made reference to a "Rosa McCauley." I was a Jenkins, but that last name sure did ring a bell. The wheels of my mind started turning in ways that went beyond thoughts of what I read; the book described what this Rosa McCauley had done to make herself known and why she was celebrated. I could hardly wait until I got home from class that day. As soon as I could get my mother's attention, I showed her the page from my book and asked, "Mom, your name was McCauley. Is this Auntie Rosa?" What an interesting conversation that was!

Auntie Rosa had gotten to know me, too. I was around her pretty regularly when I was growing up in Ann Arbor, a city just about forty minutes outside Detroit, before I became an army brat living wherever my father was stationed. But I guess Auntie Rosa figured she would leave it to my teachers to do their jobs—she never gave me any of those come-sit-on-my-knee lessons about history or what she had done in Montgomery. As a matter of fact, when we saw Auntie Rosa, she was always more interested in what was happening in our lives than she was in anything else. I've heard it told the same way by one family member after another—she didn't talk about civil rights or try to make herself seem important; she usually tried to change the subject if younger relatives asked her to discuss her own heroics. A lot of us have different thoughts about why she preferred to keep quiet on this topic when she was in our private company. My theory is that she just wanted us to be kids and not feel any unnecessary pressure because of her celebrity. I can understand that she was being considerate, maybe even more than we realized back then; if she had bragged about herself to children, we might have bragged about it, too. She wanted us to feel free to be individuals, to grow into ourselves and become who and what we were destined to become.

There was one thing she never shied away from talking about: our potential.

She taught us that anyone can do great things, although she never forced us into that role, either. She just wanted us to be clear in our understanding that how far we went in life, and the direction we took, was totally within our control. I think Auntie Rosa saw this message as especially important because she had lived through an era when there were constant restrictions on her potential, and constant reminders of why she wasn't expected to accomplish much for herself. Outside of her home and immediate circle, around every corner Auntie Rosa found herself face-to-face with enforceable laws and explicit rules about what she was or wasn't allowed to do. It's easy to take for granted that times have changed so much, most of us can't even imagine a society that actually operated this way, but Auntie Rosa was born into that world, and she witnessed it. She didn't let it overcome her, and she didn't want us internalizing the thought of there being a limit on our success.

When we went to her house, she'd greet us, help us take off our jackets, and we'd talk about whatever new and interesting developments were happening in our world. The conversation was always about us rather than about her. When I finally was able to break down her wall while visiting with her one day, I got her to share more than she ever had with me before. Interestingly, she still did nothing more than skim the surface of her civil rights activism. Instead, she rewound her memory reel all the way back to when she was a young girl. She told me that her favorite pastime was reading, and she talked about the trips she would take, sometimes walking long distances, to get to a book. When she wanted to read, she said it became an obsession she had to follow. It wasn't always easy since she grew up in rural areas with no library nearby, even if it had been one that opened its doors to people of color. Somehow, Auntie Rosa was able to make friends with some of the white kids in town now and then, and she told me how they would sneak books out of their homes to share with her. She even read books that had been thrown away. It was as if Auntie Rosa just had a special knack for finding things to read, and she would absorb herself in any subject. I am fortunate to have picked up that same love of reading that she developed. She wasn't a well-educated woman, but she purposely exposed herself to whatever sources of written communication she could find. It was a passion that added to her development throughout life.

The last time I got to see Auntie Rosa was right before I started

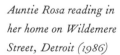

Auntie Rosa reading in her home on Wildemere Street, Detroit (1986)

high school. She wasn't as well as she had been, and I heard her faintly say my mom's name, "Shirley." Then she hugged her real tight. That was a touching moment for me, and it made me feel good for my mother, knowing how much Auntie Rosa had meant to her throughout the years. It had been an important relationship for me, too. Growing up with Auntie Rosa's influence enabled me to become self-confident, and my life has been deeply enriched because of her. I wish I could have another opportunity to let her know how much I appreciated her, but at least her legacy is still out there for me, and for everybody, to embrace. Her bond with her family isn't something that is widely known, but our memories of her will be passed down like treasure through future generations. We cherish her.

We continue her fight.

—PAUL

Starting Again

I really had put a lot of my life on hold. I didn't look at it as a bad thing, but, like plenty of other parents—mothers, in particular—I just adjusted to the demands of family life, once that time came. It was necessary, since my husband had chosen a military career that pretty much dictated the way for all of us. We would live where he was stationed and move when he got new assignments in new locations. This isn't a life for everybody, as you might imagine, but I felt that my job was to support my husband and make the very best out of it. When our first child came along in 1975, I was anything but disappointed, though I was also caught off guard. I felt unprepared. With all the transitions, it soon became more like a secondary thought that I could still have a vision for myself and how my individual future would take shape. All sorts of major ongoing developments demanded my attention, and I hadn't even turned twenty years old.

One day, Auntie Rosa came to visit while we were living out of state. It was maybe June or July, and my son was just a few months old. I didn't realize it at the time, but I was experiencing postpartum depression. For someone who had never been a biological parent before, Auntie Rosa seemed to have knowledge only a mom would possess. She was patient with me and supportive in every possible way, reminding me to take my vitamins and rest as much as I could. It was fairly basic advice, but these were things I had never had to think much about doing before. Just a couple years earlier, I was in high school, not even taking full responsibility for myself. I would need to follow Auntie Rosa's suggestions now if I was going to keep up the energy and strength it would take to look after an infant and still do my part in a marriage.

It might have been some of my aunt's seed-planting that got me to refocus later on. After years of struggling, while still maturing as a woman the whole time, my marriage wasn't able to survive. But now I had more children and even more responsibility. I was experiencing life as a full-grown adult, and I'd soon be experiencing it without a partner. This was a lot to think about, since I'd

taken the leap directly from being someone's daughter to someone's wife, and from being someone's wife to someone's mom.
What had become of Shirley, the person, in the meantime? Early
on, Auntie Rosa told me to rest and take care of myself to preserve
my body and mind. She didn't want me overstressing to the point
that I'd be no good to my family. It was time to venture out now
and explore how I could do the most good for me. In the '90s, I
went back to school to pursue a college degree.

I had the usual challenges of managing a work schedule
and finding time for class assignments and homework—all the
growing pains and twists that come with being what they call a
"nontraditional" student. It wasn't always easy, especially with
mouths to feed in addition to my own, but I pushed my way
through it after committing myself to the goal of earning a cap
and gown from the University of Kentucky. The only thing
missing at that point were the smiling faces of my parents, who I
know would have enjoyed the fact that I'd reached a new mile-
stone. Like she so often did, Auntie Rosa offered her best effort
to stand in the gap.

In 2000, Alabama's Troy State University was the latest insti-
tution to honor her, with its Rosa Parks Museum. The building
would showcase historical themes that dealt with Auntie Rosa's
time in Montgomery and other aspects of the equal rights struggle. As a graduation gift, Auntie Rosa sent for me to attend the
museum's groundbreaking. True, it wasn't Jamaica, or Hawaii, or
even Las Vegas, but the privilege of being there for such a major
tribute, out of the many she received, felt just as exciting. Adding

Defiant, acrylic and oil on burlap, by Shirley McCauley, 2004

to the experience, I would take part in the ceremony itself. All of the effort it took for me to reach that moment felt more than worth it. I had found myself, started a new race, and reached the finish line, with more goals in sight. Sharing the joy of our achievements together made the time at Troy State with Auntie Rosa that much sweeter.

—SHIRLEY

Earning My Wings

I like it better on the ground. Even all these years later, I'll still drive if I have a choice. But this time, the invitation came straight from Auntie Rosa. She wanted me to go on a trip to Connecticut with her, and I had never been on a plane before. She had a speech to give, and she was going to visit some family, too. My mother wasn't able to make it for some reason, so she talked about it with my father, and they all decided it would be a good experience for me.

This was in the '80s, so I was only about fifteen. They knew I had a fear of heights.

"I don't mess with planes," I protested.

"There's nothing to it," Auntie Rosa said. "All you do is lie back, relax, and you're there before you know it."

When you've got Rosa Parks and your parents pressing you to do something, what choice do you have? Pretty soon I had my bag packed and it was time to head out to the airport. That day came a lot faster than I wanted it to, but Auntie Rosa had the last word.

"Boy, come on."

So that was that.

Now, I had to put on my game face. She was my aunt, but I had to remember I was with *Rosa Parks*. She wasn't afraid, so I wasn't going to be. It was a mind thing. We got to Detroit Metro Airport, boarded one of those little jets, and got up in the air. We sat in first class, and soon the food trays came out. They gave us a couple strips of steak, but I noticed they were taking hamburgers back to second class.

"Can I get a hamburger?" I asked the flight attendant. But I couldn't. I guess they only had a certain number of meals for all the passengers, so I was a little upset. I looked out the window and saw the little dots and lines on the ground. Didn't like that, so I looked back inside the plane. After a while, we were landing. It went like Auntie Rosa said it would. The next day, we got on the plane and flew back. This time, we were in second class. Auntie Rosa was sitting right next to me and she fell asleep, so I just followed her lead. It wasn't long after we woke up before the jet landed.

It was worth the experience to spend that time with her and be a part of the things she did. It made me glad I was able to "man up" and not miss out because I was too scared. I probably would have always wondered what the trip had been like if I didn't see for myself. And I can't say I wasn't glad to be on the ground again once we got back to Detroit, but even though it didn't turn me into a big fan of planes, being with Auntie Rosa gave me confidence that I could face a challenge.

—ALAN

Lasting Impression

Auntie Rosa felt the direct weight of racism in one form or another for more than half of her long life. I don't mean just knowing there was discrimination and that there were a lot of people who didn't like her skin color; I mean she saw intolerance shown in ways that personally affected her from one day to the next. Whether it was the Ku Klux Klan, bus segregation, or hate mail she received many years after she got arrested, bigotry revealed its face to her over and over again. As much as my family loved her, we know there were probably people who hated Auntie Rosa until the day she died.

I once heard a story about the first time she ever encountered the sickness she would spend most of her life trying to cure. On a trip to a rural store one day when she was growing up, my great-grandmother Leona took her daughter along. Not knowing any better, Auntie Rosa started to chat with a little white girl about the same age. Maybe my great-grandmother was distracted for a minute, because I can't imagine she wouldn't have pulled Auntie Rosa to the side to avoid trouble.

Now it was too late.

"We don't play with niggers!" the white girl's mother said, snatching her away.

This reaction had to be explained to Auntie Rosa in a way a child could understand. It's sad to think about how she must have remembered that day every time she even thought about being friendly with another white child for a long time afterward.

She shared other stories with me, too, each one making her life a little more interesting; each one giving me another reason to admire her. She helped shape my entire outlook on humanity and sculpt my character as a human being. Looking back on my entire life, I've come to suspect it was people like her, my mother, and my godmother who contributed to my curious spirit as a seeker of truth and peace and as a creator of my own philosophy.

Largely because of Auntie Rosa, I have learned to walk in

love and be mentally free from any prejudice, patronizing, or racial discrimination. I learned, rather, to always search within myself to move past tendencies to outwardly judge others. Being raised partly in Southern California during the 1990s also helped my siblings and me to indiscriminately choose friends while being ourselves, a priceless gift for any child to enjoy. But California will always have other significance in my life for the simple reason that it was also the place where I would record my first memories of Auntie Rosa. She was visiting with good friends in the sunny hills of Los Angeles, and I was seven years old. Walking into the very grand furnishings of Leo and Geri Branton's home, I remember feeling that they already knew and loved my brother, sister, and me, but I didn't recognize them at all. Soon my mother was urging me to go into the kitchen where Auntie Rosa was making lunch to say hello. It felt as if I was about to meet a character out of a storybook, literally, and I was slightly intimidated, having never formed my own bond with her during those years of my young life when she was in Michigan, which seemed worlds away. I had this curious feeling as I stepped onto the kitchen floor and walked closer: there she stood with her back turned to me.

"Hey, Auntie Rosa," I managed to say.

She happily turned around with that beautiful smile and told me how glad she was to see me again. She talked about how much she'd missed our family in a way that could only be expressed by someone who'd loved us even before I really knew what love was.

Sue, with Whitney, Broderick, and Auntie Rosa

That first hug I received from her is one I won't ever forget. Her embrace made me feel like we had never been strangers and, truly, we hadn't. After that, I always took full advantage of opportunities to see her, and I cherished the time we spent together. From our meeting that day to all the others when we sat down to talk, she became a constant shining star and inspiration in my life. It was her initial greeting and welcoming presence that warmed me. First impressions are the ones that last.

— BRODERICK

Motivational Speaking

I was going through a rough period.

I had been laid off from my job at General Motors again, and I really wasn't sure how I would make it this time. If you've never found yourself unexpectedly without employment, even for a short while, I'm able to say from experience that it can truly shake up your life. Unless you're able to survive off your own personal savings, it's hard to adjust to the sudden loss of income when you're someone who lives from month to month, like most working people do. If you've got a family depending on you, the pressure is that much greater.

That's the situation I found myself facing in the 1980s. I needed help getting by, but both my parents were gone. My brothers and sisters were all part of the working class, like I was, and they had bills and obligations of their own. So even with such a large family, I didn't have an advantage once I'd spent my last paycheck before the layoff started. I'd already borrowed from Auntie Rosa a couple times. She was still like the third parent to me that she had been for as long as I could remember. My mother seemed to disappear a lot when I was a child because of all her hospital trips. At my young age, it just seemed like she vanished and Auntie Rosa and Grandma would magically show up. Auntie Rosa had also been around every time our mother had another baby, and there were nine of them after me. I remember her rocking chair, and how I fought with my siblings over who was going to sit in it. So it still felt natural for me to lean on her if I felt like I had to, because she had always been willing to share what she could.

I didn't mean to take advantage of her kindness, either. I just needed help again. The thought of asking Auntie Rosa for more money didn't give me a great feeling, even though she had provided it freely when I first approached her for loans. I swallowed my pride, sure that it was the only thing standing between me and the bit of relief I needed. But I was surprised this time when I called Auntie Rosa to ask if she would please lend me fifty dollars.

She said no.

I hadn't counted on the conversation going that way. Instead of money, what Auntie Rosa gave me was a stern message: "You were raised to be strong," she said, "not what I'm seeing. Stop feeling sorry for yourself. You'll think of something."

She was abrupt in that way she could sometimes speak, and her words stung me, but they were true—I *had* been feeling sorry for myself. Our parents, along with Auntie Rosa, taught us all to have a strong work ethic. You do what you have to, whether it's through a job or education, and you do it for as long as it takes. When you get it right, that's when the work is done—not when the clock shows a certain time or the calendar hits a specific date. That's how we were taught. My father worked until he couldn't work anymore, retiring only when he got into a hospital bed and dying soon after. He never had any extended period of relaxing or traveling the world to sightsee and celebrate how he would finally get a break from grinding away, year after year. Work was a way of life for him and had been since he was a little boy. I never heard any of the adults in my family complain about their labors. I believe they were teaching us the same attitude they had been taught by their parents.

Remembering this and letting my aunt's words sink in got me refocused. I still needed that fifty dollars and I wouldn't be able to get it from the source that I was counting on, so now I had to brainstorm a bit. *You'll think of something*—that's all Auntie Rosa gave me to work with! What other skills did I have aside from my job at GM? I thought about it. . . . I could paint. Put up wallpaper. Clean. Sew a little. There were things I'd picked up from my parents over the years.

I called around to a few people I knew, advertising myself for hire, and it wasn't too long before I reached a friend who needed her kitchen and dining room painted. I did better than fifty dollars—I made a hundred the next day. And things took off from there. In just a short time since that phone call I made to Auntie Rosa, I had more odd jobs and assignments than I was able to take on. It was a whole different outcome than if I had simply gone to my aunt's house to pick up the money and then spent it. That would have been the end. I'd be out of cash once again and fifty dollars deeper in debt. I'm so glad Auntie Rosa reminded me of the people I came from and what I was made of. She had transformed from nurturer into motivator exactly when I most needed the motivation. If she hadn't fussed at me that day, I think my pity party would have just continued. As generous as she had always been, she had the wisdom to know that, sometimes, holding back was a better solution.

—ROSALIND

Heeding Her Call

We'd just gotten home from a family reunion at Boblo Island. Once in a while, Auntie Rosa would decide she wanted to see the entire family together, and this was one of those times. We heeded her call. With our parents and Grandma all passed away, it felt good that we could still say there was truly a head of our family. Someone we all respected not only because of her elder status, but because we knew Auntie Rosa genuinely wanted what was best for each one of us. It was the summer of 1991 and, once again, I needed my aunt's help.

My marriage was in trouble. It had become a source of constant fighting and stress. Our issues with each other were like those of many couples, the conflicts and struggles that sometimes happen when two people with different personalities get together. However, the clashing between my husband and me had become toxic. So much so that we probably couldn't separate the original sources of our tension from the petty, less-worthwhile things that had started to trigger our huge flare-ups at the time. Whatever the spark in this blowout I had with my husband not long after Boblo might have been, it turned into something that equaled a raging fire. We fought terribly. And by the time I thought of the first person I knew I had to call, I was already crying uncontrollably. These were tears that came from some of the deepest emotional pain I had been going through, pain that was forcing itself out of me, showing no mercy in the process. It was the kind of hurt that doesn't just pull, but rips at you. I cried a flooding river, and it wasn't until I could start to recognize the sound of Auntie Rosa's soothing voice that I even started to calm down.

I don't really remember a lot of her words since so much time has passed, but I remember her comforting me just like I know my own mother would have, just like I needed and had known she would. Auntie Rosa wasn't just our family matriarch; she was a mother to us in every sense of the role. In my biological mom's absence, it wasn't just being sentimental to say she was now the only mother I had. I do remember her telling me I had "some decisions to make" about remaining in a marriage that had turned so volatile. I'm sure those words weren't issued lightly, since Auntie Rosa strongly believed in traditional husband-and-wife relationships. She wasn't one who would hastily tell anybody to end their marriage. That was an area where she could speak from personal experience after having Uncle Parks as her husband for almost forty-five years, even as they went through life-changing events that would test the patience and devotion of the most loving couple. Neither of them had been perfect, but they found ways to last together until Uncle Parks took his last breath, and she kept on loving him even long after that. So although it might have come across as common sense advice from anybody else, it carried a lot of weight for her to suggest the thought that it might not be wise to stay with my husband. We hung up the phone and, that night, I slept on her words of wisdom as I tried to heal from the day's deep battle scars.

The next morning, I got up planning to take care of my daily duties. I had young sons and responsibility, so no matter how drained I felt, there wasn't time available for me to sit down and lick my wounds. What caught me by surprise was hearing someone at the door after I'd seen the children off to school. I answered and saw my oldest sister, Mary, outside.

"Come with me," she said. I gathered myself and followed her out to the car where she explained that Auntie Rosa sent her over to check on me. I guess my state of mind the night before had really worried Auntie. She had used her normal, calm tone in our conversation, but she was careful not to let me know that hearing how upset I was had upset her, too. Mary gave me similar advice to what Auntie Rosa had said. I needed to think about whether my marriage should continue, my sister told me. It must not have been a secret to either one of them that my husband and I hadn't gotten along well for some time. I walked around downtown with Mary, which I know she thought would do me good. The air and change of scenery just for that short time gave me a chance to clear my head.

I didn't make a decision the next day, but I gave a lot of thought to what I heard from Auntie Rosa and Mary. Only I knew what I had gone through and how much more I could take. As it turned out, it was more than a dozen years before my husband and I divorced in 2006, the year after Auntie Rosa passed. I wanted to try

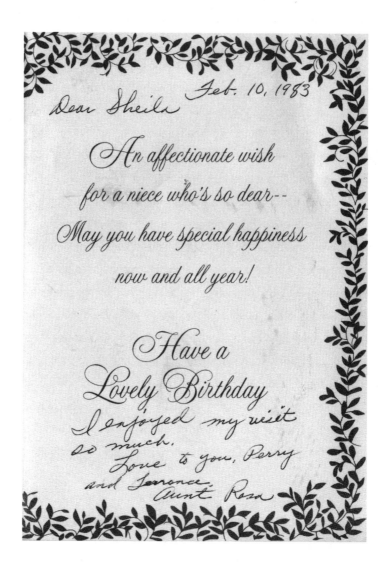

Feb. 10, 1983

Dear Sheila

An affectionate wish
for a niece who's so dear--
May you have special happiness
now and all year!

Have a
Lovely Birthday
I enjoyed my visit
so much.
Love to you, Perry
and Terrence.
Aunt Rosa

to give my sons a stable home for as long as possible, and I don't regret that choice. My ex-husband was a good father, and we're on friendly terms today. What I'm always thankful about is that Auntie Rosa had an ear to lend me, and that she even provided her own follow-up care, in the form of sending Mary to talk with me the next day. She didn't have the solution to our problems all the time, but Auntie Rosa helped me see how much just being willing to listen could mean. I hope I'm as effective in that way with my loved ones as she was with hers.

—SHEILA

Show-and-Tell

Even with all her other obligations and undertakings, it seemed that Auntie Rosa made a conscious effort to stay involved in our family's daily lives as much as possible. She was, hands down, the most devoted, loyal person you could ever meet. On one of many instances, against the backdrop of a flawless California day in 1993, she proved it.

My older brothers and I woke up to get ready for the short walk to Bear Gulch School. Sean and Ryan were always teasing me, basically just for being a girl, and today was no different. Then Sean's attention turned to something important, at least, by elementary school standards. I heard him complaining to our mother that he had a show-and-tell assignment due just a few hours later. The problem was that he couldn't figure out what he should take to class. Sean seemed torn choosing between his favorite video game or his roller blades. Although I was even younger, I recognized that my brother was always serious about schoolwork. For him, show-and-tell was a *big deal.*

My mother encouraged him to hold off on making a decision until just before his two o'clock class, so Sean agreed. Mom was planning a surprise: she asked Auntie Rosa, who was in town, if she'd visit the school. When I got home from my shorter day of class, Auntie Rosa was there waiting with Mom, and we all made the trip back to Bear Gulch together. We found Sean's room, and Auntie Rosa walked in just in time. My brother was beyond surprised. Tears filled his eyes as silence fell over the room. Better than any version they'd ever read, Auntie Rosa shared her firsthand story of the day she refused to give up her bus seat in Mont-

Left to right: Susan, her daughter Whitney, and Auntie Rosa on Easter Sunday in California

gomery. The teacher, Mrs. Ayers, pulled out her camera as the kids listened without distraction, having had no idea this show-and-tell would be one they'd probably remember for the rest of their lives.

Needless to say, Sean received an A for his assignment and he impressed a lot more classmates than he would have with his video game or roller blades. At my young age, I learned something valuable, something that has stayed with me all these years—to never forsake the little things that might actually be big things to people we care about. Sean's tears of joy weren't only because he was happy to see Auntie Rosa; they were because he never imagined he was important enough for her to do something so special for him. By her example, she taught me that encouragement and support can be as simple as showing up for the people we love.

—WHITNEY

Guiding Light

This was one of those rare occasions when we were in the same room and still had some physical distance between us. It was also one of the times when I got to see my aunt in a new light—literally. I had moved to suburban California, and Auntie Rosa was visiting with friends nearby. On this day, sometime in the early 1990s, I joined her in Los Angeles to make the most of whatever time she had available before journeying back to Michigan.

One of the advantages I lacked by living out of town was that access to her in the way I had been accustomed, that access most of my family had enjoyed for our entire lives. Fortunately for me, Auntie Rosa made friends with the Brantons, Leo and Geraldine. Leo was a prominent civil rights lawyer who had counseled Angela Davis and several Black Panthers, people who had taken the freedom fight to new levels. He also represented major names in entertainment, like Nat King Cole, Dorothy Dandridge, and Miles Davis. Leo was just one of the many fascinating types of professionals whose paths crossed Auntie Rosa's. He and Geraldine had hosted her for dinner at their house one day when an author writing about Auntie Rosa's life escorted her to that gathering. Two weeks after that visit, Auntie Rosa began a fall migration ritual: in late October, she started making annual trips to Los Angeles to stay with the Brantons until spring. They had a comfortable suite on the second floor of their house in Lafayette Square, and they welcomed her. She'd spend winters giving talks and laying the foundation for a West Coast office of the Rosa and Raymond Parks Institute. More than thirty years of full-time Detroit living had conditioned her to hate the cold that spread over Michigan as autumn crept in, so this ritual retreat continued for a decade. Not only did Auntie Rosa have time to get away from the frigid weather, she enjoyed some relaxing moments sitting out by the Brantons' pool or occasionally satisfying her appetite with Gerry's home-cooked gourmet meals.

Maybe it was because I wasn't directly involved in this particular conversation that I was able to notice it as Auntie Rosa chatted contently with the Brantons. They'd long gotten into the habit of trading war stories and weighing in about the country's direction, socially and politically. Whatever the topic might have been on this day, I was less intrigued by the words they exchanged than by my aunt's appearance. From my vantage point across the room, I saw a soft glow around her, a light that exuded from her outline. Was this the source that had always attracted so many people into her presence? As strange as this might sound, I was truly witnessing her *inner glow*. I saw the bright spirit of what made her the person she was and, momentarily, I was captivated.

I sat watching her as she spoke in her low, even-toned voice, laced with a distinctly Southern accent—the same one she and my father both used in conversation. I'm sure she paid me no attention as she continued talking, but I'm glad I was watching her at the time. Yes, it was Los Angeles and the weather out was bright and attractive. I could have dismissed the image surrounding Auntie Rosa as just a backdrop, like in a movie scene. I could have told myself I was just seeing the warm, golden light of the California sun coming through the window. But I think it was much, much more. The sun had shone lots of times when we were together, and my mind had never played those tricks on me before.

That wasn't the only time I looked at Auntie Rosa, silently admiring what I saw. A lot of you have seen it, too—the way her face beamed in photos when she smiled. It's almost like her light grew even brighter as she got older. I've never seen an image of Auntie Rosa smiling that didn't move me. Even in the most casual of settings, her gentle shine could be noticed. She didn't have to be around important leaders or in front of huge crowds, but at the big ceremonies and formal meetings with dignitaries, I'm sure they all caught it, too. I don't believe it was just having the opportunity to meet a legendary figure that made people talk about it like it was one of the biggest highlights of their lives; it was the pleasantness she showed them in all of her many encounters. I was in awe of how those less close to her were drawn as powerfully as we all were. It seemed that everyone wanted to be in her presence, whether they were performers, politicians, social activists, or just family and friends.

I would always ask her for beauty tips on how she kept up her appearance as she gracefully aged. "Auntie Rosa," I'd say, "your skin is so clear and beautiful. What are you doing that's different?" Once, she told me she swallowed a spoonful of olive oil every morning, a regimen that I dutifully began following. But I think I knew then, and understand now, that majestic, timeless beauty shines from the inside out, not the other way around. The natural health care she gave herself only highlighted what was already there, making her goodness visible to human eyes. What I saw on that day in Los Angeles was a source of peace she always nurtured within herself. She didn't need a forceful kind of energy in order for it to be felt.

For Auntie Rosa to have a glow like I witnessed after she had been the target of so many vicious daggers was a thing to behold. Like a glorious seal, it revealed itself and I'm sure she couldn't have suppressed it, even if she'd tried. This was a glow of peaceful triumph. Her personal light could never shine as it did if she hadn't been able to claim victory over all the things that had ever been set up to defeat her.

—SUSAN

What's in a Name?

A night that changed Detroit forever was also a night that would eventually secure one person's memory in the city's collective mind. The interesting thing was that no one, including Auntie Rosa, would have ever made the connection between those violent and, for thousands of residents, life-changing events and her own immortalization almost a decade later. No hint was given that it was this person's name that would be used to symbolize a rising from the ashes. Wise as she was, not even that woman could have predicted it.

IN 1965, a new member of the U.S. House of Representatives was elected. John Conyers was named congressman for Detroit. An army veteran, he had spent time down in Alabama, organizing for voting rights, though he was born and raised in the city that he successfully campaigned to represent. He knew the struggle that was being carried on throughout so much of the South, and he would later reveal the mentality he held about discrimination and victimization toward certain Americans by writing bills that reflected his concerns over disenfranchisement, hate crime, and related forms of oppression. Yet for all that his legislation did to help millions of citizens, there was no more significant thing he did for us than hiring Auntie Rosa. But this hadn't been an act of charity. Conyers knew Auntie Rosa before she moved to Detroit, and they had crossed paths when he traveled her way on Southern Christian Leadership Conference business. After she got to Michigan and found out he was a congressional candidate, she started showing up at his campaign meetings. Pretty soon she was volunteering and helping to get Conyers the ballot support he needed to earn a victory. Returning the favor, he offered her a job as a staff aide once he was voted in.

Two years later, he found himself standing on top of a car under the blanket of night. The only light not coming from moon, stars, or street lamps came from the glow of flames stretching from building rooftops toward the sky. Arson ruled without mercy. Mass break-ins and store thefts followed close behind. This was evening number two in a madness that would spill out like the blood of the injured to stain Detroit for several days of fierce rebellion—the result, generally, of a community's repressed resentment over racism and police brutality at a time when the population swelled with people of color but didn't expand with their representation in government or law. More specifically, it was the fallout from a hypertense moment just before daybreak on July 23, 1967, when cop aggression was met with resistance of the variety that spread, quite literally, like wildfire.

Detroit Police coordinated a strategy that would get them inside a private club on Twelfth Street, right above the Economy Printing shop. The company was within walking distance from Auntie Rosa's house at the time on Virginia Park, where she lived with Uncle Parks and our grandmother. United Civic League of Community Action was the name identifying the upstairs meeting space, but officers decided it was really a "blind pig" that served alcohol after two o'clock in the morning, the legal cutoff. With no idea by either the guests of the establishment inside or the officers taking positions outside that they were about to clash in one of the ugliest uprisings of the twentieth century, the action jumped off: squad members made their move, and it wasn't long before they were bringing a procession of eighty-two people from the building out into the open air to be booked into jail and face charges.

Things didn't go so smoothly.

A crowd started to form, watching what was happening, and the people quickly began to grow resentful of the officers; soon they numbered a couple hundred, which was far more than the police had been prepared to confront. Somebody threw a bottle. Then a brick blasted through the back window of a police cruiser. At the time, there were only 193 officers patrolling all of Detroit—a city of more than a million—and bedlam was about to make its journey from the typically calm blocks surrounding Auntie Rosa's house all the way down the rugged sidewalks and commercial lots decorating Fourteenth, Linwood, Dexter, and Grand River Avenues. When the first of what wound up being hundreds of stores started burning, we were still safe in bed Sunday morning, expecting to make our way to Auntie's for a visit later that afternoon.

SYLVESTER WANTED this little blue '66 Mustang. He was the oldest and ready to experience some of the freedoms of being a young man. But something happened with the car payment arrangements, and Sylvester couldn't drive it anymore. Father wound up taking the Mustang off his hands, and that was the vehicle used to shuttle us around when he wasn't driving his pickup. The truck was usually reserved for Father's handyman jobs. Since the Mustang had more space and there were no seatbelt laws in those days, five or six of us would pack ourselves into it like sardines. Father crammed as many of us as he could into the rear seat. He even gave us a positioning method: lean forward, lean back, forward, back. Nobody sat shoulder to shoulder. We angled our bodies in the opposite direction of the person sitting next to us so our legs could serve as armrests for our siblings and our torsos weren't as jammed. It wasn't the most comfortable or safest way to travel, and probably only added a few inches between us, but this was the kind of creativity that was sometimes needed to manage a big family. McCauley-style geometry, you might call it. Good thing we were all skinny.

Either nobody had paid much attention or nobody had felt the need to worry yet about what started on Twelfth Street when we piled into the Mustang to ride to Auntie's. The uprising was only a few hours old then, and Father must not have been concerned enough about it to change our plans, if he knew anything was happening at all. By venturing out to Auntie Rosa's, we had left the safety of Deacon Street, miles away, on the city's southwest edge, and driven right into the fast-growing danger. Uncle Parks and Auntie Rosa would never have hesitated to warn us that we should stay home if they knew what was happening practically right in their backyard. Most likely, even as word got around that there had been a big disturbance with the police, they would have expected it to be put under control, as most of the neighborhood did early on. At some point during our visit, though, the TV was turned on and there was a bulletin. The fires were spreading, and things had turned deadly serious. Before the night was over, a city curfew was issued, telling everyone to be off the streets between nine and five o'clock the next morning.

Well, Father wasn't about to wait for a curfew to get his kids back to the safety of home. We all gave our usual hugs and said good-bye to Auntie, Uncle Parks, and Grandma before stacking into Mustang formation again. Not even then did we know just how bad things were becoming, but our caution level quickly rose toward fear as Father drove to what became our first block in the road ahead. This wasn't the kind made out of wood that traffic workers put in the street, either—it was a blaze at the end of Dexter. Father wheeled the car in the other direction, and there was a fire down that street, too. We all got quiet, like we knew he would want us to be. This time, tires could be heard screeching as he turned around again and navigated a way out of the chaos until we were on our way to the house. That was the end of our day's adventure, but that night in the city was perilously long.

DURING THE SECOND DAY Detroit burned, it was obvious that the curfew hadn't slowed anything down. Angry black men and youth were joined in the streets; now the crowd was mixed with opportunists who knew the blue uniforms were hopelessly outnumbered. It wasn't solely about police harassment anymore. It was about getting whatever satisfaction one felt entitled to—material, emotional, or otherwise—from a system that had always denied. In the sultry summer temperatures, vindicators could be spotted strolling up Twelfth Street with fur coats draping their bodies like regal robes. Others seized the moment to feed themselves and their families by raiding and relieving the A&P supermarket's shelves of canned goods and meats. Elsewhere, marauders hauled off jewelry, televisions, and radios as if they were plundering a village that had been conquered in battle. Detroit had become the village, and little was spared.

Unsatisfied, possibly, with the takeaway of anything valuable in a neighborhood shoe repair shop, still another mob turned rapturously violent, dragging the old man who owned it out into the street and beating him without mercy. Somewhere in the midst of it all, Congressman Conyers emerged. He and Reverend Nick Hood, the city's lone black councilman, had braved their way into the chaos, hoping to reason with the simmering rebels. Posted on the hood of a vehicle, Conyers spoke through a bullhorn, saying, "We're with you, but please, this is not the way to do things! Please go back to your homes!" His message had no effect, just as Detroit Tigers star Willie Horton's words fell on deaf ears; he had left a home game that night and wound up on Twelfth Street, still in uniform, failing to make an impression on the crowds that took over there. He was a baseball player, not a negotiator, and if anyone had been starstruck enough to heed his wisdom, it wasn't apparent by the numbers that remained.

The governor declared a state of emergency, and now four hundred state police officers and 7,300 National Guard members were there in the eye of the storm. But many of the reserves were ill prepared to respond to such a major rebellion. In numerous cases, these were young men who had only joined the Guard to keep out of the Vietnam draft and avoid the war overseas. Like the feeble Detroit Police force, they quickly proved themselves incapable of containing the violence. They set up at a recreation center near our house, probably because it was far enough from the hot zone that they could feel safe to retreat there and figure out an approach. On top of everything else happening, there were reports of snipers, and even some firemen had been shot at for trying to put out the ever-present flames. We could see the armored jeeps outside the building that served as the Guard's command station, but none of this was enough. On Tuesday morning, 4,700 airborne soldiers in full battle gear descended on the Motor City. It wasn't long before assault vehicles, including tanks, rolled down public streets, and when Wednesday came, the forces combining to restore order achieved some results. Three thousand people were arrested that day alone, with so many in custody that police garages, gyms, and city buses all had to be used to hold them temporarily.

By the time the rebellion ended, forty-three people had died, with thirty of them killed by law enforcement or military. The very first to lose his life was a forty-five-year-old white man shot by a Fourth Street market owner after the man stole several pairs of shoelaces, cigars, and a few packages of tobacco. Close to five hundred people, including firefighters, police, and military, were injured during the week, and 2,500 stores were looted. Of the 1,600 fires reported, retail businesses like Charles Furniture, Kresge, and Red Robin were burned completely to the ground. Thoughtful in his analysis of what had occurred was Governor George Romney, who spoke of expressway construction and prior urban renewal that left poor folks "bulldozed out of their homes," with few prospects for relocating. Many of the displaced residents were virtually forced out into the Twelfth Street section of the community, he said, "so when that incident occurred, it was a spark that ignited the whole area."

As large as our family was, all of us had managed to keep ourselves safe from harm, including everyone at Auntie Rosa's house, so close to the flashpoint of it all. In contrast, the city faced many years of recovery, with race relations being a significant part of that healing. Yet it wasn't the last time buildings in Detroit would burn, like they did a year later when Dr. King was assassinated.

When it felt safe to venture out, Father took one of us riding in the back of his truck, where the vanishing view of Livernois behind it showed store furnishings strewn across the middle of the road. This was then known as the "Avenue of Fashion" for its shopping outlets, but it was dotted, like much of the community, with charred structures.

Come the next decade, someone who all of us knew well was going to be used to promote the city's revival.

COLEMAN A. YOUNG was elected Detroit's first black mayor in 1973. As a native of Tuscaloosa, he shared the birth state of our parents and Auntie Rosa. He also shared Auntie's background in fighting for equality and advancement. A lot of us were there at the small public ceremony in 1976 when he announced that Auntie Rosa's name had been chosen to replace Twelfth Street. From then on, it would be known as Rosa Parks Boulevard. Mayor Young thought Auntie Rosa deserved the honor since she was a part of the neighborhood. With the damage from 1967 still evident, the new street name could be seen as a fresh start for the people and businesses that had suffered.

Traffic was blocked off, and there was a seating area for spectators observing the event. When the new sign with Auntie's name was unveiled, it was one of our proudest moments. She said a few words, and there were a handful of reporters present to relay the news. From what had been the city's most devastating episode, Auntie Rosa was chosen as a symbol of forward momentum. That was one more of the numerous times when a trait we admired about her became public knowledge: she was resilient.

Now there is a street to prove it.

—SHEILA, ROBERT, AND ROSALIND

The True Price of Fame

Auntie Rosa was no stranger to the White House. She had been welcomed and affectionately received by presidents for decades, maybe even before she, like much of America, ever dared to imagine herself electing one who looked like her. As history would reveal it, the woman who lived to see so many groundbreaking changes in society missed witnessing Barack Obama's historic 2008 victory by just three years. Now, here we stood in the presence of President Obama himself, looking up at a blue drape in the Washington, D.C., Capitol Building's Statuary Hall. Beneath the drape was the attraction that had brought about fifty of Auntie Rosa's relatives together that day. We traveled from various parts of the country to attend the unveiling of a life-size statue sculpted into her image, making Auntie Rosa the first black woman to be honored with a monument in that highly esteemed corridor. Not only was the president there for the occasion, but lawmakers from both parties, like Nancy Pelosi, John Boehner, and Harry Reid, participated in the ceremony. Baseball legend Willie Mays sent his personal greeting, congratulating us in a

ABOVE: *At Statuary Hall in the U.S. Capitol Building for the unveiling of the statue dedicated to Auntie Rosa (2013). Left to right: 1st row: Susan McCauley, Sheila McCauley Keys, Shirley McCauley, Rosalind Bridgforth; 2nd row: Nikki, Faye*

BELOW: *Left to right: Senator Mitch McConnell, Sheila McCauley Keys, Senator Harry Reid, President Obama, Speaker of the House John Boehner, Representative Nancy Pelosi*

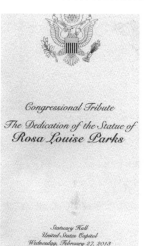

Congressional Tribute

The Dedication of the Statue of
Rosa Louise Parks

*Statuary Hall
United States Capitol
Wednesday, February 27, 2013
11:00 a.m.*

letter. It was the thrill of a lifetime to share one end of a decorative tassel with elected officials who acknowledged our aunt as an American hero and pull the golden rope to reveal her bronze image. That first look at the finely chiseled form of Auntie Rosa sitting in a dignified pose, much as she had during those days of Alabama protest, left our chests swollen with pride. Our family matriarch was making history again as the moment was broadcast all over the world and captured in photos taken by news and Web media.

Later, we clicked our own cameras as we stood near the statue, absorbing the happiness and memories of that February day. The itinerary included a visit to the White House with President Obama. He had spoken at our aunt's funeral, where celebrities like Michael Jackson and Cicely Tyson joined a mall-size church filled with mourners both familiar and unfamiliar to us. We appreciated the way Obama acknowledged our family when he took the microphone as a still widely unknown Illinois senator. He quoted a scripture, "The Lord is near to all who call him, to all who call on him in truth," from the Book of Psalms, before reminding everyone that our aunt had never held any corporate position or public office. "And yet," he said, "when the history of this country is written, when a final accounting is done, it is this small, quiet woman whose name will be remembered long after the names of senators and presidents have been forgotten."

Our trip to D.C. took place only a few weeks after many of us had attended a major Detroit-area celebration observing what would have been Auntie Rosa's 100th birthday on February 4.

February 25, 2013

Nancy,

I am sorry for missing the statue ceremony. I have had eye surgery recently and traveling isn't so easy. I hope you understand.

I know who Rosa Parks was and I understand what she faced. We had the same thing in Birmingham, only we called them trolleys. They had placards that told you where to sit. I was too little to understand why it was that way. That's just how it was. I am grateful to have lived long enough to see things change.

I worked on some comments, (below), to share with you. I want you to know what my feelings are. You can share them or you can save them. They are for you to keep.

Remembering Rosa Parks

"Most times, change doesn't happen fast. Most times, it happens bit by bit, little by little, one person's actions inspiring another. Rosa Parks simply did what was natural. She was tired, so she sat down. And that simple act sparked outrage and that outrage spread and one person's actions inspired change. Today, when we look back, we sometimes forget what a brave thing she did. We forget that natural wasn't always so easy to see.

"Today, we will try to remember. We will try to remember to be careful about what we think we see. We will try to remember to do the natural thing, the right thing, the kind thing. We will try to remember to encourage change when it serves justice. And, today, we will remember with admiration, the simple act of a brave woman. We will remember, we will honor Rosa Parks."

Thank you,

Willie Mays

That was when the U.S. Postal Service unveiled the stamp bearing Auntie Rosa's likeness. A full day of activities, speeches, choir performances, and other tributes had been scheduled for the general public, bringing hundreds of people to the Henry Ford Museum. This celebration would have qualified as, by far, the biggest party anyone ever threw for Auntie Rosa. She would have been truly overwhelmed by so much attention, and looking back on the amazing month of February 2013, that's the thing people who never had the privilege of knowing her should understand. Neither statue nor stamp would have ever been more important to Auntie Rosa than continuing efforts to improve the world we live in.

She would appreciate being remembered and being loved, and she would appreciate it sincerely, but this appreciation could never replace her sense of pure values. That Auntie Rosa became the object of so much admiration during her lifetime was more than she ever expected; that she is still the object of so much admiration in death reminds us just how much she would want personal praise to be given its true perspective. She would want everyone who buys her stamp to buy it with the confidence that they could do remarkable things, just as she did. She would want every visitor to the Capitol who ever gazes upon her statue to also gaze upon a vision becoming reality of communities where the poor prosper and the suffering prevail. From every gracious senator, member of Congress, and legislative aide we met in Washington to the least noticeable face in the crowd of spectators paying tribute at the birthday observance, our aunt would have viewed them as equals. Auntie Rosa knew how wrong people had been to dismiss her and those she represented, and she knew how much she had been underestimated at one time.

She was a woman who showed leadership without ever once, in nearly 100 years of living, holding a formally designated title or rank. She would become great simply by acting on what she believed.

—SHEILA AND SHIRLEY

Vision

· ·

I want people to get off the bus and step into the future.
Realize that you have the power to do what is right.
You don't have to wait for someone else to do it for you.

—ROSA PARKS,
conversation with niece Shirley McCauley

Tuskegee, Alabama, was her place of origin.

Of course, Montgomery later claimed her. Then Detroiters yelled, "She's ours!" Eventually, Rosa Parks was loved throughout the world. But the place that produced legendary educator-activist Booker T. Washington and the legendary Tuskegee Airmen kept producing legends. Born into Jim Crow segregation, Mrs. Parks was, like the others, an unlikely candidate to change the system. Her parents separated when she was only seven, and she later quit school to care for her sick mother, Leona. With no more support from their father, she and her brother, Sylvester, teamed up to work in and out of the house, attempting to make up for the shortage of resources.

It wasn't a life that forecast Mrs. Parks' destiny of traveling the country, meeting mayors, heads of state, and even the pope. It wasn't a life that forecast complete strangers wanting to hug her, kiss her, or ask for her autograph. In any case, she would be mostly unaffected by all of this. What changed the

forecast of who Mrs. Parks would ultimately become was her
powerful optimism and perseverance. As the family shares
here, part of what made the poor granddaughter of ex-slaves
a global legend was her ability to see a better future for her-
self, her family, and generations that followed. Mrs. Parks'
ability to embrace new ideas and opportunities for personal
growth well into her senior years gave her a rare vision that
had an impact on more lives than she would ever realize.

Institutional Values

The Bible says we can't "despise small beginnings," and you
could say I was starting pretty small at this time in my life. I had
been through a few struggles, and I was living with my brother
and his family in 1981. He had just gotten out of the military, and
we both needed a job. At the same time, Auntie Rosa was making
her small beginning: she was stepping out only a few years after
Uncle Parks died to start the program that was going to carry
both of their names, the Rosa and Raymond Parks Institute for
Self Development. It worked out that we needed to make some
money, and she needed some help with maintenance.

The program was inside a church at Fourteenth Street and
Grand Boulevard in Detroit. We cleaned about four or five classrooms, and we performed janitorial duties around the building.
Auntie Rosa wanted to use the institute to teach students about
what she had done, about their history, and to take them on learn-

ing trips. But this was still in the blueprint stage. There wasn't a lot of money, and we made less than a couple hundred dollars a month. She had a few people running the program for her, but the problem was there were too many chiefs and not enough Indians. We were the Indians. A lot of times, when payday came around, we got a song and dance instead of a check. I remember seeing Auntie Rosa there a couple times, but she wasn't real hands-on in the day-to-day operation. She was still doing her speaking engagements, and she had her job with Congressman Conyers. I think she was too trusting.

Well, I got a lot out of just knowing that I was helping her build her dream. Auntie Rosa was so unselfish with the things she did, and it was a good feeling to be there for her, even on those hard, no-pay days. She was starting from the ground up, and I knew she was going to do everything she could to make it a lot bigger. After about two years, the Institute was taking shape, and they found a new place. Auntie Rosa knew we had all those payroll issues now, and she wasn't going to take advantage of us. When my brother found another job, he broke the news to her and she understood. She went one step further with me: Congressman Conyers' brother had a car dealership and she got me a job working maintenance there. Even though Auntie Rosa was always willing to sacrifice for others, she never held anybody else back.

None of our family is with the Institute today, but those early days taught me a few things about dealing with people, and about myself, too. I learned that you have to be thankful for what you've got, no matter how little it is. A little bit of something is better than nothing at all, whether it's money or help. Auntie Rosa had a goal that didn't go as smooth as she wanted, starting out, but her small beginning grew to be what she wanted in the end.

—RICHARD

Auntie Rosa and Upward-Facing Dog

I remember going to Auntie Rosa's house in Virginia Park in the late 1950s. I would regularly help her and Grandma with the chores and housecleaning. These times have left me with fond memories of being in their company. Auntie Rosa was always busy writing, reading newspapers and magazines, or watching the news. She always kept informed. She had *Jet*, the *Michigan Chronicle*, and newspapers that had been delivered from down South. It impressed me to see how she kept up with current events and how she was interested in continuing to educate herself. I liked the fact that she always developed her mind and that she wanted us to learn, too. She always listened to other people's ideas and points of view, even though she was strong in her own opinions.

For as long as I can remember, I wanted to be an artist. When I let Auntie Rosa know this, she encouraged me to fully pursue this goal. It was like she could always find the best in us, no matter what. Being around her helped build my self-esteem, especially at a time when the world was filled with so many signs and messages about why children like me weren't as worthy as others.

Auntie Rosa had long known better, and she did whatever she could to remind us that the only limits were the ones we set for ourselves. She always wanted to know how I was doing in school and in life, generally. When we went to church, people treated her like she was walking a red carpet. I liked the way she carried herself.

"This is my nephew," she would tell the other members, who shook her hand and asked for her opinions. This made me feel good.

She was organized and would keep her books and papers stockpiled. If she were alive and well today, she would definitely own a laptop computer. That might seem hard to imagine—the lady in all those black-and-white photos using modern technology. But it's not a stretch for me, because I saw how she took on new tasks. She was never intimidated by anything just because she wasn't familiar with it. Should that be surprising to learn about the lady who sparked a yearlong bus boycott to overturn an entire system that was designed to crush her?

Auntie Rosa was never stuck on tradition. For example, having been raised on a Southern diet, one of her favorite dishes was calf's brains with scrambled eggs. She became much more health-conscious late in life, at an age when many of her peers were so set in their habits that not even a doctor's warning might have convinced them to change. We would go to the Cass Corridor Food Co-op together and share ideas about nutrition. I came to realize that Auntie Rosa had interests that not too many people knew about. Her receptiveness always left me pleasantly surprised. This was especially true when she decided to join us at yoga classes. She really enjoyed it. Most people could never picture the Mother of the Civil Rights Movement doing "upward-facing dog" or any of the other poses, but the older Auntie Rosa got, the more it seemed she evolved.

My fondest memory of her was in 1984, shortly after our first daughter's birth. It delighted me how Auntie Rosa warmed up to our baby. By this time, we had drifted apart somewhat, since the earlier days when I spent so much time around her and my grandmother. Although she gave me attention when I was in her company, it was still the 1950s and grown-ups didn't do much fraternizing with children; in this way, Auntie Rosa was no different. Now, my younger siblings, who interacted with her while they were maturing in the 1960s, had a closer relationship with her. So when our daughter came along as part of a generation even further removed from that of my father's and aunt's, I thought she would be somewhat distant. Again, I was pleasantly surprised by how affectionate and engaged Auntie Rosa became with Zakiya. She taught me that you have to give of yourself. That's what she always did. When you have children, this is especially true. Even though we were like her children, I think the movement was her first child. That's what she dedicated her life to, and it taught me there are greater things in life than ourselves. Auntie Rosa's vision taught me that you've got to have lofty ideas. You have to think. That's the only way you can find out who you really are. And those ideas, like Auntie Rosa's, must be oriented toward helping people. My mother also taught me this. If she had somehow been able to remain here with us, I think the public would've been surprised by the person who was still becoming Rosa Parks. She was always adapting to the changing world.

—ASHEBER

Poetry in Her Motion

She stands motionless, the palms of her hands pressed together in a prayer-like pose. Slowly, she raises them above her head.

Breathe in.

Breathe out.

Well into her senior years she has only recently begun practicing yoga. Splendid silver hair gives her away as the oldest student in most of the classes she occasionally attends with family, but she doesn't care. She's reached a point when she considers herself a student of life. Her level of growth isn't tied to her age, and she likes it that way.

Now, her palms are flat on the floor. A slim leg moves forward and bends as she pushes the opposite foot back, balancing her weight. She switches legs. Concentrates.

Deep inhale.

Deep exhale.

Eventually, she learns the movements and yogic principles well enough to practice alone in her home. She'll answer the door wearing yoga pants. The exercises help clear her mind, the stretches keep her body limber. In her space on the floor, she

Sheila and Auntie Rosa.
Acrylic on canvas, by Nestor Madalengoitia, 2013.

takes sanctuary, be it at a studio under the voice of an instructor or in the sunlight of her living room. Inner peace and clarity have always been important to her.

Poses like the "lotus," "warrior," and "upward-facing dog" weren't common where she came from. Now she knows them. She hasn't lived in India, but she respects its ancient traditions. She isn't a Buddhist, though she is definitely enlightened. She is my Auntie Rosa.

Namaste.

—SHEILA

When Auntie Joined the Angels

Everything was organized at the last minute. My mother got the call from Auntie Rosa on a Monday, asking if I could be in Provo, Utah, as soon as possible. It was totally unexpected. It was 1999, and Auntie Rosa was making a special appearance on the television show *Touched by an Angel*. The CBS series, which was at the height of its popularity, starred Della Reese, Roma Downey, and John Dye as three spirits taking journeys down from heaven to inspire humans at crucial points in their lives. The writers and producers of this particular episode had cast Auntie Rosa as herself; she was to visit Monica, Roma Downey's character, to offer words of wisdom and solace as Monica experienced what life would have been like if she'd been African American in a small Utah town.

To say I was honored and surprised to be chosen by Auntie Rosa herself as an "extra" is an understatement. My role was to help "Rosa Parks" as she stepped onto and off of the bus, lending her a strong arm to lean on as she encountered Monica and the other characters. I had been a participant of the "Pathways to Freedom" tour Auntie Rosa sponsored through her institute, and I was a pretty seasoned traveler. I would be the envy of my friends and classmates after flying across the country to the set of a TV show! But first, I had to channel my energy—to have a "Rosa Parks moment," which is what we call it when there's no other choice but to be exceptionally brave—and summon confidence at the ripe old age of thirteen to make my first plane trip to a place where I'd never been, and with no adult chaperone. I was truly relieved to see another "Pathways to Freedom" veteran, my friend Ramia Davenport, waiting when I made it, bags packed, to the airport's gate. Having a friend to travel with quelled my anxiety.

I think my mother might have been even more excited than I was. She drilled me on my itinerary to make sure I wouldn't wander off the face of the planet. Ramia and I kissed our parents and boarded the plane together. On Wednesday, we were in Provo. Things went smoothly as I made it to the set. I found out the legendary John Ritter would star in this episode with Auntie Rosa. He played a sheriff's deputy working with a black partner to deal with racial violence in their town. I'll always remember the morning when I met Mr. Ritter in the hotel's gym. Some other young men and I talked with him at length. It was another unbelievable aspect of the trip for me. Of course, none of us could know that, just a few years later, Mr. Ritter's many fans would mourn his passing.

I am one who believes all things are in divine order and that the universe unfolds as it should. There are no coincidences or mistakes. I truly believe my Auntie Rosa insisted that I be a part of this event for reasons that will be revealed to me someday down the line. I didn't develop a passion for acting, but I did develop an appreciation of that memorable time with her, even though I was sad to see a decline in her health since we'd last been together. Our family lived in Georgia now, and I was looking forward to one of those special encounters when Auntie Rosa talked and I listened, but she was very quiet, even tired, as the hustle and bus-

Susan's son Sean's ninth birthday party

tle of a network TV crew swirled about her. I'd treasured those summertime moments between "Pathways to Freedom" program events, spending breaks alone with my aunt, or dining privately with her in a quiet place instead of eating the catered lunch with a hundred other program participants and staff.

She didn't have many lines in the episode. One memorable thing is what she said to John Ritter's character when he told his partner that he knew "where we stand," following an honest conversation. Auntie Rosa peered out from the doorway of the bus: "Yes, I think you do," she said. "You're standing on God's side now." It was fitting for her to deliver that message. On a show about angels, *she* was chosen to point out who was on "God's side"! That was more perfect than viewers of the show knew, since Auntie Rosa had a true gift for seeing good in all people.

—SEAN

A Special Kind of Recovery

In grade school, I heard about a woman who sparked the civil rights movement by refusing to give up her seat on an Alabama bus. Only later did I find out that woman was my aunt. Like the rest of my family, I felt honored. While, in the early years of her settling in Detroit, our parents, Auntie Rosa, and Uncle Parks had to help one another make ends meet, time saw things gradually improving for her, financially. I saw less of Auntie Rosa because her speaking engagements increased. Now and then, she would invite Father, me, and some of my siblings to those annual NAACP dinners that became a sort of tradition for all of us. Of course, she knew practically everyone there and would tell us who everybody was. As I got older, I would make some bad choices and suffer a personal setback that changed me into someone who I definitely was not.

IN THE 1980s, I started experimenting with drugs and alcohol. This went from recreational use to full-blown addiction. My siblings still loved me and were concerned about me, but with both my parents gone now, there was one remaining elder whose acceptance I feared losing. Would Auntie Rosa shut me out of her life? I never wanted to be a source of embarrassment to her, and it hurt me to think about my addiction causing this to happen. It was something I hadn't ever imagined taking hold of my life, but now drugs were my reality, and the battle was daily. Sometimes there wasn't even a battle. I was addicted, and addicts often give in.

However it came to her attention, Auntie Rosa didn't call to give me a lecture. She never once made me feel the guilt that I know would have overwhelmed me if I had heard her say things like, "I'm ashamed of you," or if she'd reminded me of all she went through, only for a member of her own family to blow the opportunities created by her sacrifices. Not only did Auntie Rosa spare me the hurt that would've come from hearing such statements, she hardly ever raised the topic of my addiction at all. She must have just known, intuitively, how to support me through that terrible time. Or maybe she just loved me too much to treat me with rejection, like some mothers—but maybe not quite as many aunts—would have loved me. In spite of my irresponsible ways, Auntie Rosa occasionally hired me to help organize her papers and do other odd jobs, like moving boxes. Even in those days, it was always a treat to be with her. She welcomed me into her home, offering me whatever food she had. We'd talk about politics and the family, things that made me feel relaxed and comfortable.

I even traveled with her to Alabama for my great-uncle Anderson's funeral in 1985. Up until that point, we had never spent so much one-on-one time together. We talked a lot during the fourteen-hour drive, and I remember eating with her at a truck stop in Tennessee. She talked if you engaged her on a topic, but as usual, she shied away from the one that came to my mind, now that we were both together in the South. *Yes, I'm the lady who refused to give up her seat, but we're here for dinner* was the message she communicated without actually using those words.

Uncle Py's funeral in Alabama.
Left to right: Robert McCauley Jr. (Auntie Rosa's uncle), Auntie Rosa,
Robert D. McCauley (Auntie Rosa's nephew)

The trip was time well spent. Back in Detroit, I even remained a welcome guest at the NAACP dinners. And Auntie Rosa never put me down or slighted me. Ever. The closest we really ever came to talking about my drug problem was when she told me, "Play the cards you've been dealt." I understood this to mean she knew I going through tough circumstances, but that I should continue the struggle. This was like a lifeline for me. She often would tell me, "I think about you all the time." Her spiritual enlightenment was far above anything I'd ever seen.

TODAY, I WORK as a mechanic for the post office. I have not been a substance abuser in twenty-three years. Although I did find professional help and started attending AA meetings in 1982, when I remember Auntie Rosa's quiet and gentle support, I don't think even a professional drug counselor could have been much more helpful to me. I'm grateful she lived long enough to see me "play the cards" and win. This was one of Auntie Rosa's greatest gifts: a way of seeing things—and people—not only as they were, but as they *could be*. She saw that her nephew needed time and inspiration to fight the biggest battle of his life. She believed in me. I thank God for the time I had with her.

Amen.

—ROBERT

Queen of the Road

Back when she was still active and keeping busy, before she took on more assistants and handlers to help with her affairs, family members would sometimes travel with Auntie Rosa if she had to go out of town. Whenever we could attend a speaking engagement with her, she made sure the family had a table at the front of the room, and she would make us stand up as she introduced us to the audience. It wasn't us they cared about, of course, but Auntie Rosa seemed proud to share the spotlight. She was nearly always the main attraction wherever she appeared, and she was surrounded by many people who wanted to see her and get as close to her as they could. They saw Auntie Rosa as living, breathing history, and she was approachable, consistently.

Once, when Auntie Rosa was going to a speaking engagement, some women in the group that would become her staff wanted to see her glammed up. They told her to put on fur and wear a lot of makeup. She was firm in her refusal: "I don't wear fur, I don't wear makeup, and I don't wear jewelry," she told them. How would that have looked? She was entitled to nice things as much as anyone else, but what message would it have sent for a woman who wanted people to continue working toward equality to show up dressed like a well-off socialite? Besides, even though she didn't wear color on her face, or accessorize, she was always very, very meticulous about her appearance. I'm so glad she made her own decisions about the public image she presented. It was one of

the many times she showed how important it was that people follow their own minds.

I went out of town with Auntie Rosa, and I would occasionally
meet her on weekends in between some of her trips. I soon began
to realize that her schedule was too hectic for me. Even though I
was a young and energetic woman, her travel dates increased to a
point that, to me, they felt overwhelming. How did she handle it?
At one time, it seemed that Auntie Rosa was literally living out of
suitcases; giving talks, having lunch and dinner appointments
with all sorts of people, and then getting back to her hotel room to
pack and head back to the airport so she could start the next whirl-
wind trip. She was doing all this without even taking naps! It was
hard to believe she found the energy, but this was around the time
that Auntie Rosa worked hard to build a legacy she could pass
down to the community, and she was determined.

She was a woman on a mission, and neither her age, nor the
way she dressed, nor how much work she had to do were going to
be factors that she let put her behind schedule. While she could
have rested for all the remaining years of her life and basked in the
warmth of her family's love, she chose to go out on the road and
continue spreading a message of peace as often as she could. She
chose to help create a foundation that young people who were still
benefiting from her sacrifices could use to grow stronger.

Some gave her street signs. Auntie Rosa gave scholarships to
keep youth off the street.

Some gave her community awards. Auntie Rosa gave community programs.

Some gave her appreciation gifts. Auntie Rosa gave gifts of opportunity.

As hard as I know she worked during those years, I can only guess it was pure dedication that kept her from running her own body down. Today, when I look around and see all of the lives her efforts touched, I understand why she couldn't rest. Even if she had driven herself into the ground completely, I don't think she would have had it any other way. I think she saw it as her calling to give back to the world, and to do anything less for as long as she had the ability would have betrayed her true purpose.

—DEBORAH

The Next Generation

None of us can remember a time when our aunt wasn't loved all over the world. Although we didn't have the pleasure of growing up with her in the same house, or having her help raise us like she did our parents, Auntie Rosa's bond with us was just as strong as a grandmother's bond with her grandchildren. Most of our generation of McCauleys were born after 1970, the first family members to live in America after the end of the civil rights movement. We woke up to a whole new day when sitting anywhere on the bus, no matter what part of the country the bus traveled, was a citizen's right, not some legal offense. To our peer group, "colored" was a description of the crayons we used, and "white" was just one of those crayons. All of us who are now adults and young men and women know that racism still exists. Some of us have experienced it. Yet we owe so much of what changed for our good to the work and commitment to change shown by people like Auntie Rosa. We are the true beneficiaries of the freedoms they envisioned and took hold of, knowing we would one day follow where they had walked.

Equal rights weren't her only blessing to our lives. While we might not have all those dozens of memories of eating at her dinner table, traveling to her events, or learning sewing lessons from Auntie Rosa that our parents have, she showed interest in each of us as often as she could through talking and through sharing her time. On several occasions, just by showing up and sitting in the crowd, she planted seeds of motivation for us at special school, community, and church programs. Her appearances always added to the highlights. At Peter's Rock Missionary Baptist Church, a set of eyes looked out from the front of the sanctuary, where the pastor was preparing to start a baptism ceremony. There was Auntie Rosa's familiar face, next to her niece Rosalind, watching as Rosalind's son Alan awaited his holy dedication to God. Surprising him, Auntie Rosa had found the time to witness this, missing service at her own church that day. Another time, she showed up at Al's graduation from Southwestern High School. This time, he had known she was coming; what he didn't know was that she was the keynote speaker who would be introducing him as part of the class of 1989.

It was impressive enough that she kept track of our parents' birthdays and spoke to them regularly; that she could follow all of their children's different activities and achievements was incredible. Auntie Rosa made a way to show she cared. Her hugs were loving, and her Southern hospitality made you feel welcome at her home. Her handshake was firm and communicated a grip that let others know she was confident in who she was. She was always on the move and had a lot of energy, and she always wore a smile that lit up everything around her. Auntie Rosa had a great sense of humor and was always in a good mood. She loved a good joke and didn't mind having one played on her or helping to prank someone else.

There were occasions when we were actually accused of using Auntie Rosa's name as part of the prank. For some reason, kids in particular refused to believe we could be related to her. After seeing her as larger than life, it must have been hard for them to imagine her having a family at all, especially one with relatives sitting in the same classroom where they learned every day. Having been in Cleveland for a while after moving there, Lonnie and Urana asked to see Auntie Rosa. They had let some classmates at Moreland Elementary know she was their grand-aunt, and now they were being harassed about it—so much that they came home crying. A month later, Auntie Rosa showed up in Cleveland to speak to the class. She gave a talk, and her message, which seemed to fit the reason for her invitation, was "Remember who you are. Don't let anybody stop you." The day after her visit, the student body had a whole new respect for Lonnie and Urana. Even the teachers were in awe.

It was the same for Terrence when he graduated from St. Cece-

lia Catholic School and Auntie Rosa showed up for the com-
mencement. Her attendance made for a spectacle, with people
flocking to see her, even though it was supposed to be a big day
for all the students. Apparently, she was just used to it. She'd
pleasantly say, "Okay," to everyone who approached her, asking
if they could embrace her or grasp her hand. That made a lot of
people's day. She was so accessible, and it became easy to see what
Auntie Rosa meant to people outside our family; even those who
were our age and hadn't witnessed firsthand what she did as an
activist were excited to be close to her in the flesh. A lot of us were
there to witness Auntie Rosa receiving the Congressional Medal
of Honor in Washington, D.C., so watching the way others idol-
ized her got to be a normal thing. After seeing her greeted by
nationally known politicians, it was obvious how much she was
revered.

At her Washington memorial service, there was a similar envi-
ronment. We sat in the church behind Senator Ted Kennedy and
Oprah Winfrey, and we even visited the White House. Republi-
cans, Democrats, and independents all paid respects in ways that
seemed genuine. Auntie Rosa had never been elected to any public office, but she was treated like a high-ranking official. Her
protest in 1955 made an impact on the government that these lawmakers now ran. Because of her and other soldiers, they knew
now that they represented all people as equal citizens. Auntie
Rosa helped change the way congressmen, senators, and party
leaders did their jobs so they would serve the interests of our generation and the ones after us.

Auntie Rosa at her grandnephew Alan Bridgforth's graduation from Southwestern High School in Detroit, Michigan

Through her we learned quiet strength. She wasn't constantly giving pep talks and lecturing us. Sometimes just being in her presence was enough to give you the essence of who she was. Everything about her was so subtle, but like gentle water that erodes rocks over time, her force couldn't be denied. Reflecting on the way we knew her, and the way she touched all of us, it's understandable that she became a spark that set people's hearts ablaze. We would like to think that we have inherited some of her noble spirit. We hope we can instill her same humility, determination, and self-sacrifice into our families.

As the bearers of the McCauley name, most of us accept it as an obligation to carry onward in ways that would make Auntie Rosa proud of all of us and reflect the work she did while she was alive. We're grateful that the same blood she had runs through all of our bodies, and that we saw her in the private light few other people could, as well as observing her in the public's eye. She was the model of grace, regardless of who was watching. She was the model of dignity, even when she faced less-than-dignifying circumstances. Realizing that we fall into the same peer group as the grandchildren of Malcolm X, Medgar Evers, and Viola Liuzzo makes it even more clear that we have to represent the best of Auntie Rosa, as those heroes would surely want younger generations of their families to represent the best of them. Those three brave activists all died before turning forty, while Auntie Rosa lived more than twice as long, which means we have fewer excuses. We know what she would have wanted us to do because we

At Terrence's graduation from St. Cecelia Catholic School in Detroit.
Left to right: Aunt Mary-Ann Brown,
Sheila McCauley Keys, Auntie Rosa, Terrence Keys

had so much time with her to learn the assignment. If nobody had ever known her name outside the family, Auntie Rosa was still a woman who we would all choose to emulate because of the help and support she taught us to give one another. It just happens that she was the Rosa Parks who gave help and support that went beyond her biological family. She was the Rosa Parks whose impact could be felt on countless corners and in numerous communities, and who sent ripples of her ambition spreading like weeds across the widest acres. Auntie Rosa had an effect that made almost everyone she encountered better for having known her.

These are traits we claim as legacies to us. She was good in her heart, and that's what everyone saw when it came out in her behavior. That same goodness is in all of our family members. It's not weakness. It's what let Auntie Rosa move among all classes of people, from sharecroppers to international leaders. What it really represents is power, and Auntie Rosa showed us how to use this kind of power to make positive changes in the world, and in all of our lives.

—ALAN, LONNIE, TERRENCE, THOMAS, WHITNEY, AND BRODERICK

THE CONTRIBUTORS

ABOVE: *(left to right)*
1st row: Richard McCauley, Alan Bridgforth; 2nd row: Rosalind Bridgforth, Najma Wilson; 3rd row: Asheber Macharia, Marc McCauley, Zakiya McCauley Watts, Sheila McCauley Keys, Robert McCauley; 4th row: Terrence Keys, Lonnie McCauley (Photo by: Joel Boykin)

LEFT: *Shirley McCauley*

Left to right, front to back: Susan McCauley, Whitney Carnes, Broderick Carnes, Sean Carnes

Paul Jenkins

Thomas Keys

Deborah Ross and Rhea McCauley

ACKNOWLEDGEMENTS

With gratitude and appreciation, the authors recognize the following for their various contributions of support: literary agent Susan Raihofer, attorney Larry Pepper, Cynthia Zajac, Jennifer Treece, Linell Allen, and all the generous people who kindly lent their names in endorsing this book. Lastly, thanks to Joel Fotinos, Sara Carder, Joanna Ng, and the wonderful artists and staff at Tarcher for believing in the vision for *Our Auntie Rosa*.

ABOUT THE COAUTHOR

EDDIE B. ALLEN, JR. is the author of *Low Road: The Life and Legacy of Donald Goines* (St. Martin's Press, 2004). An award-winning reporter and freelance journalist, who has covered such world figures as President Bill Clinton and Rosa Parks, Eddie's newspaper and Web media contributions include the *New York Times*, Reuters, Associated Press, BET.com, *Detroit Free Press*, *Toledo Blade*, *Orlando Weekly*, and *Philadelphia New Observer*. Eddie lives in Detroit, where he is producing an adaptation of the book *Low Road* as a feature film. A Rosa Parks Scholarship recipient at age seventeen, Eddie's college journalism studies led him back to Mrs. Parks, full circle, in 1995 as a reporter covering the violent, widely publicized break-in to her home. He would later write about Mrs. Parks' nationally televised funeral as well as various aspects of the freedom struggle that carries her footprint. More than twenty years after they met at his scholarship presentation, a photo of Eddie with Mrs. Parks still hangs in his family home.